Spinach Soup for the Walls

Spinach Soup for the Walls

Finding my spirit in Africa

Lynne Harkes

A record of this publication is available from the British Library.

ISBN 978-1-907203-46-6

Typesetting by Wordzworth Ltd
www.wordzworth.com

Cover design by Titanium Design Ltd
www.titaniumdesign.co.uk

Printed by Lightning Source UK
www.lightningsource.com

Cover photo by the author

Published by Local Legend
www.local-legend.co.uk

Disclaimer
Any references to people mentioned are not intended to represent specific individuals, but are composites of many characters encountered in several countries.

To my extraordinary family, Neil, Olly and Joe.
It is my privilege to be part of your team,
to grow and to learn together.

"When you stand and share your story in an empowering way, your story will heal you and your story will heal somebody else."

—IYANLA VANZANT

Acknowledgements

With infinite thanks to my lovely dad, Alex Harkes, to my mum and sisters and to the realms of angels, for never giving up on me; also to Steph, a wise and literary head on young shoulders whose unwavering support has helped me to move mountains, and to Pam for an enduring friendship that has spanned continents.

My gratitude also to Nichola, Jen, Shirley, Maddy, Calista, Rowala, Dawn, Lesley, Jacqui, Barbara, Aileen, Nicola, Zoe, Karen, Catriona and Paula for being who you are and helping me to see the bigger picture whatever the drama unfolding.

Special thanks to Nigel Peace of Local Legend for his generous help and support with this book.

About the Author

Lynne was born in Edinburgh where she now lives and works as an artist. Her paintings are vibrant and colourful, expressing the true beauty of nature that we often miss in our everyday world.

She has travelled extensively due to her husband's work, which saw the couple relocate every few years. In her writing she conveys powerfully the highs and lows of such a travelling life from Nigeria to South America, from Oman to the jungle of Gabon.

But despite the privileges of this no-madic life, it can also be tough and chal-lenging. Lynne frankly describes her personal struggles and her transformation from despair to a spiritual path and a new way of living.

"To know ourselves," she says, "we do not have to walk through blazing fires..." Rather, it is through seeing the simplicity and beauty of nature and of everyday life. A new lightness has emerged in her mind and in her painting. In both her writing and her art, she inspires us to "see the remarkable in the ordinary".

www.lynneharkes.com

Contents

Chapter 1
Leaving Oman

A sprig of basil, washed, disinfected and given a new lease of life from its former grubby home and elephant dung fertiliser, was now beginning to spread its bruised wings and sprout roots in a recycled tomato tin on the patio. Only close inspection revealed the army of ants that were also now setting up residence, traipsing through the lumpy soil on a mission to turn the leaves into a delicate, nibbled piece of green, aromatic lace. Even at this early stage, it was completely unfit for human consumption. Perhaps it was telling me something. Everything familiar to me was going to be entirely challenged in this place.

Gabon, West Africa and 144 days under the belt. I'm trying hard to tone down my obsession for liking things in meticulous and controlled order. I need to embrace the wonders of this jungle around me and continue with the job of improvisation. Many days I struggle. I've even begun to resent the dog's little grey water dish, transformed now to a makeshift pen-holder. It is filled with a handful of felt and biro pens and sits incongruously beside a historic looking company-issue telephone on a thickly over-varnished windowsill, looking silly.

A few weeks earlier, when I placed it there, I'd been so thrilled at my ingenuity. All the childhood years of watching Blue Peter had paid off. Surely someone not privy to this training would have overlooked the possibility of transforming a dog's drinking vessel into a stationery item. I'd once been lucky enough to receive a Blue Peter badge, in recognition of a pencil sketch of John Knox I'd entered into a competition, comprising small strokes and moody shading. I remember it had flowed from my hands with unexpected ease. I never missed the art section and had soaked up the skills that were now so invaluable in this empty jungle house with such limited resources. I'd had a good training for the life here. My husband had been transferred to this strange jungle enclave as an engineer for a large energy company and the plan was that we would settle ourselves into the unusual life and whatever Yenzi Camp living presented for the duration of the four-year posting.

This was our tenth relocation over the years, six of them having us leave Britain for foreign shores with freight containers bulging and varying levels of enthusiasm and trepidation. For much of our nomadic life, a solid friendship and respect for each other had eased us through the stress and the challenge presented to us by this chaotic lifestyle. At this point, however, relations had become strained and awkward, with both of us becoming emotionally withdrawn from each other. Occupied fully with the preparation for Gabon, we'd partially pushed aside our differences. Only time would tell whether, in this jungle setting, we'd be able to recapture the essence of love and happiness that our marriage had lost.

I had admiration for the pens in the ex-doggy water dish, bearing so well the humiliation of being placed in such an inappropriate container. They were doing a better job than me, struggling to overcome my awkwardness and resistance to my environment. They stood proudly erect, queuing patiently for action, plastic warriors waiting in eager anticipation, knowing that only a message of the highest frivolity would require the services of the green and red and, more than likely, the trusty black with its head furry from over-use would again be enlisted for duty. This was not a time for frivolity, after all. If only there was something to write on and some news, any news, of our 40 ft container and belongings arriving.

Months earlier we'd left Muscat, Marmul Street and home for the last five years, with our Jack Russell Travis in tow and the little grey water dish filled to a safe aeroplane take-off level. I'd watched Travis in his cage ascend a steeply inclined conveyor belt into the belly of the luggage compartment and had been relieved we'd not been too generous with his in-flight drinking ration. My husband and I had been living in Muscat, our second spell of residency in the delightful Sultanate of Oman and location number six of his career. This posting had arrived on the tails of one of life's tumultuous periods and, with emotions fragile, we had both kept our hands firmly by our sides, unable or unwilling to reach out freely to forging new friendships amongst our fellow camp dwellers.

This posting in Oman had passed as a somewhat sugar-coated shell bereft of filling and had been almost unrecognisable socially and emotionally to our previous stay there, surrounded by friends and our tribes of small, excited children. The fresh young couple who had headed off twelve years previously with two toddlers to embark on their first overseas post had been replaced by jaded and somewhat more cynical versions. At times during our stay, it had been a battle for me to muster up a smile, from a sea of internal tears resembling anything even half convincing.

However, the show had to go on and we had once more climbed to the top of the company's transfer list. Firstly, we were bound for a couple of luxury days in Paris, before heading south to Africa and Yenzi, a little camp in the middle of the Gabonese jungle. Our new home. For several weeks now, we'd lived with the aromas of cardboard and had already experienced a taste of how life might change, with things as we knew them being packed up, with every sickening scream of the parcel tape stretching over gaping boxes. I knew how that tape felt. I was screaming too.

"You'll love it," they'd all said reassuringly. "The company's best kept secret." Surely they couldn't all be wrong?

❋

As a creature of habit I always strive to keep things familiar and in order. From the day of unpacking, five years previously, not one thing had moved in the Marmul Street house. I always had the feeling, rightly or wrongly, that there could be no better combination of walls and furnishings than that already achieved. Working on the sort of Olympic adrenalin that kicks in when a 40 ft container's contents are deposited in your home, I knew that together my husband and I had optimised the space and there was no room for improvement. We had developed into a good team as far as emptying bursting freight containers and injecting style into mediocre company housing goes. A palpable sigh of relief when our job was done. Boxes and parcel tape could be banished for an indefinite period and life 'settled' for the next few years. We could get on with the job of living, whatever that was to entail.

Amidst the flurry of packing, the first victims to be eliminated from our Middle Eastern home and bound for the Africa container were the luxury touches: the silk cushions that perfectly united the muddy brown of the sofa with the softer shades of the rug and encompassed, so well, the rich tan shade of the armoire in the corner. Many an evening, frustrated with the poor choice of satellite TV, my eyes would wander round the room and the sight of the bristling textures and tones would make me smile. I knew I'd derive the same pleasure after this enforced separation ended and I tried to be as upbeat as possible amidst the upheaval and attempted to focus ahead. Next to go were the sparkles, my beloved bling candle-holders. Life was literally losing its shine, save for a wine glass with a tea-light burning, around which I'd painstakingly hung wired-up crystals and which shed an array of rainbow wonder dancing around the room. This would somehow make up for the daily disappearance of my other much-loved interior jewels and would symbolise a tenuous control over what at times felt like a hopeless situation, completely out of our hands.

We'd sat in a dreaded and energy-zapping limbo situation for many months. Our paper-processing for Gabon had unfortunately coincided with political troubles that had delayed the issuing of our necessary visas and entry permits. There were days of despair, turning down invitations and most frustratingly not being able to support our boys in the UK with their various needs. How long could it possibly take to make a simple continental move?

※

Paris was French and lovely when we eventually arrived. Our two sons, visiting from Scotland, were once again briefly reunited with the dog, having been too long apart. Tails wagged, legs jumped and tongues licked in recognition. Of all of us, it seemed Travis took to his European break the best. He was appreciative of pavements that cooled rather than scorched his paws, as he'd been used to in the Middle East, and French lampposts that appeared to have better stories encoded into them. After much hunting in and around the airport environs we'd managed to find an area of grass for him a train ride away and a new experience for him. Finally, after four years of life making do with blistering concrete and gravel in Oman burning his paws, he had grass to spring around on. Add to this the Parisian experience of an open-top bus tour, wrapped in my intricately hand-embroidered pashmina to warm his shivering Middle Eastern limbs, and he was visibly smiling. Could canine life get any better?

As much as we could with a four-legged travelling companion we wined, dined and took in the sights of the city, made all the more poignant by the impending travel to the heart of the jungle. There would be none of the customary cappuccino shops in our new leafy home and to soften the blow we were cappuccino-ing round the clock and taking bites of as many heavenly tartes aux framboise as possible in a 72-hour stop-over.

❋

Travis had unexpectedly arrived into our family after a fleeting but admittedly loaded "Do you ever get Jack Russells?" enquiry to the owner of the Oman city centre pet shop followed by an exchange of mobile 'phone numbers. Some six weeks later the 'phone rang: "He's here", said the excited caller. "The dog, the Jack Russell, he's here for you."

"Ok, I'll come and see him," I managed a somewhat shock-tinged reply, with my mind racing as to the best way to present the news of our impending pet-hood to my husband.

Needless to say, with a telephone earpiece still warm, we found ourselves standing in the caged-dog section of the pet store with two diminutive black, white and tan puppies excitedly vying for our affection. In the end we went for the cute one, who seemed fractionally calmer and, we naively reckoned, unaware of Jack Russell single-mindedness, more trainable than his boisterous brother with his mismatched eyes, one black and one white. We left the shop with a little cardboard box, our new addition tentatively poking his head out and beginning to introduce himself and giving us the first clues as to the awesome character his smallness concealed. It took us only as long as filling his new water dish with cool refreshing water to name him 'Travis'. A large name we thought, for a little dog. Travis was, for much of the Oman posting, the glue that kept my husband and I struggling on together and the focal point for our conversations. His arrival felt like some bizarre twist from God, a reason to have to stay together in this location and quietly to endure pains and learn some lessons from this modest canine teacher.

Travis has also taught the family much about themselves. Unlike the dachshunds we'd had as children, who used to sulk for days if we'd been away, Travis is unfailingly always delighted to see the family return from overseas jaunts and enforced separation, wagging his tail like an over-excited metronome to welcome us back. He is very certain of himself and in true Jack Russell spirit considers himself to be the biggest of dogs in his smallest of suits. Visitors to our house must be prepared to engage in his generous welcoming, as he leaps up and down towards their hands in unrelenting yo-yo fashion. The higher their hands of protests go, the fuller his jumps become. He takes mad turns, suddenly and out of the blue, running full pelt, skidding from bedroom to living room and back, free-jumping over sofas and duvets and crashing heavily into walls, utilizing our rugs as surfboards. He knows he is simultaneously breaking all house rules and is profusely mocking our restriction of dog leisure activities, but he knows too how to charm us. He'll curl up on his beanbag at our feet and sleep the sleep of the innocent as soon as he's satisfied himself with his acrobatics and the scene of devastation around us all.

Sometimes I consider that being compared to a Jack Russell is the greatest of compliments. For their loyalty and tenacity, for their fun-filled spirit and cheeky character, Jack Russells are tiny heroes who aren't ashamed to sing out their own song with the full pitch of their voice.

Jack Russells of the dog kingdom are on a par with golf of the sporting world. They both have a hidden special something that prompts you to inspect life and yourself with a magnifying glass, often exposing your weaknesses and always teaching you something invaluable. Many a time, a round of golf has forced me into deep self-analysis. I remember, years back, one particularly humiliating hole, the fourth, on a Beginners' Morning in Nigeria, with blue sky and perfect conditions.

Enthusiasm to launch the ball skywards sailing powerfully towards the hole, involuntarily made my body over-exert to comical proportions.

Instead of a graceful, effortless and controlled swing I launched at the ball with the finesse of a Wellington boot-thrower at a Highland Games event. The ball jumped in fright from its proud position atop the plastic tee and a reversal of roles saw the tee fly into the sky while the ball nestled into the depression where the tee peg once stood, making not one centimetre of forward progression. My golfing partner on the day, a non-beginner savvy of the rules of the game, loudly declared: "Now, you are NOT allowed to re-tee, you MUST hit it where it is," her precise and stern Germanic tones husky from years of tobacco. "Of course, of course," I'd managed to respond, completely humiliated.

Instead of filling lungs with deep, calming breaths and re-grouping, I took another swipe at the thing, now nestled in its little dip on the tee box and cowering from me. This would have been a difficult shot for an experienced golfer, never mind a novice like me. The ball, this time more defiant, juddered forwards and rolled off the tee box but opted not to take in any air. The shot was unlike anything I'd ever seen in the professional games shown on TV that I'd sat and watched with my dad. In fact, I'd mostly watched his thrilled face glued to the screen rather than the actual game, absorbed and delighted by the sporting entertainment. I had subliminally over the years taken in the rudiments of the game along with a curiosity about the passion surrounding this king of sports. Anyone with a level of knowledge beyond mine would have discarded the driver by now, the biggest club in the bag and with a head the size of a medium steak burger in a bun. An iron, with its more precise cutting edge, would have slipped under the ball and easily done the trick. In my panic, I'd just kept adding insult to the injury and continuing the task with an impossible tool. Seventeen hacks later, tears in my eyes and a lump the size of the ball in my throat, I eventually managed to struggle the little thing into the elusive hole. I went home mortally embarrassed and upset, to work out the mental and emotional impact of using up so many shots on one hole, managing at least to congratulate myself for hanging in there and finishing the job.

※

Life was sweet indeed and we were ready for the challenges ahead. And so, nine pieces of check-in luggage later, including an unwieldy fishing rod holder whose most important job was to contain one of my rolled-up paintings to make an instant personal statement in the new house, two cabin bags and one very excited Jack Russell, we took on Charles de Gaulle airport. We had gone to great lengths to pack carefully including attention to basic kitchen and medical equipment. We were advised to forgo the customary air freight shipment, which reputably took over four months to arrive in Gabon, and instead prepared to live from the contents of our suitcases until the sea freight arrived which was expected to take anything upwards of five months.

In addition to our mountain of excess baggage, I'd decided to exchange my city-style handbag that had looked so cutting edge in Muscat for a much more appropriate leather over-the-shoulder jungle-type bag. It was a thing of beauty, two exquisitely stitched pockets adorning the front of it for handy access to vital life-saving rainforest items like mosquito repellent and lip gloss. The whole contraption closed safely with a huge, deliciously-folded leather flap. The design was a marvel. Now stuffed to the gunnels and smelling of chicken dog chews, it weighed a tonne. Never mind the bruise that was emerging on my shoulder and the months of costly chiropractor sessions rapidly being undone, the whole thing oozed style and said "smart-sensible, stylish and practical" in every language, especially French, which I was grappling to recall from my school days and which was going to be essential for our new life in French-speaking Gabon. With a check–in that seemed just too simple for such a momentous journey we were off. The stress of the preparation and the tedium of the months of limbo were seemingly cleansed as we broke through the clouds, launched into the sky and on our way south.

The preparation for jungle life had truly been a nightmare of unimaginable proportions. There had been the measuring, the estimating and the guesstimating what it would take to make jungle life easier, more comfortable and the house more our home. This culminated in the sort of shopping sprees normally reserved for Lottery winners. Unfortunately, in our case we weren't wished on our way with the sound of popping champagne corks and paparazzi poses, with cheques the size of a cinema screen, promising our lives wouldn't change. We knew above all else that big cataclysmic changes were coming and we would never be quite the same after. It would be inconceivable to live in such remoteness and away from civilisation and not be cajoled into some sort of a metamorphosis.

Due to the remoteness of the camp we were relocating to, we'd heeded advice from people on the ground to stock up and based on this advice spent months and an inordinate amount of stress on the project. It's hard to quantify the type of decisions made and energy expended to fit out a house and buy food for meals you are going to cook for friends you've yet to make. This was at the other end of the scale from 'travelling light' and the whole experience of jungle preparation took on a horribly indulgent feel. We'd shopped and dropped, even down to the average number of light bulbs we might use in, say, a year or two. We had to consider all aspects from curtains we may fit in rooms we might have, to loo seats, cabinets and towel rails for company bathrooms that, experience told us, would almost certainly have remained well back in the previous millennium.

There was a ray of hope and a shopping high-point, namely the triumphant discovery of a paint shop in Edinburgh specialising in bespoke mixes. After great shade debates, the bemused shop assistant kindly mixed us a gloriously dark seaweed-meets-rock-festival-ground for our new African walls. It was a fabulous pot of thick gloop, shining and glossy like a nutritious spinach soup requiring only a dusting of freshly grated nutmeg and a blob of cream on top, with perhaps some fresh baked bread on a side plate. The paint was to be sneaked into a separate shipping container leaving from Edinburgh and bound for Gabon. The thought of being separated so long from that little paint can prompted us to carry at all times, from that moment on, small samples of our own special brew, carefully painted on cardboard and neatly trimmed, like some funky new perfume launch. This was to serve as a reminder that we were maintaining some faint control over the allocation and re-fit of our new abode. In reality, of course, that side of things was as ever in the hands of the company, or ultimately and perhaps more reassuringly, in the wise hands of the universe. Even the knowledge that this paint shade was several degrees away from the company's 'off-white' policy had lost some of its rebellious feel. Whatever happened, and whatever the struggles ahead, the lessons my husband and I learned from our experience would surely be ones appropriate to us and perhaps even do wonders for our personal growth.

✳

I like to describe myself as an arty type won over by simple things like finding the precise shade of sludge green to transform an up-and-coming white wall, or seeing the beauty of the colours hidden in the autumn leaves trampled underfoot. Sometimes, I have to resist the urge to pull over random strangers and point out the wonder that passes by beneath their blank stares. I have a thing lately with the little plants, which nobody intended to grow, sprouting between the pavement cracks and squeezing out of gaps in railings. Their defiance astounds me. They seem boldly to be doing their own thing, producing delicate blooms or infant leaves, which contrast so markedly with their austere backdrops. I admire them more then they know and such a sight always lifts my spirits. It doesn't seem to matter to them that due to their inappropriate location they could at any minute be plucked out or sprayed to death by noxious weed-killing chemicals. It matters not to them that they may only be spotted and appreciated by a limited audience. It only matters that they do their best to grow into their own magnificence and for however brief a time. Doing their thing is what they know and they are not ashamed. They understand that a tulip was meant to be a tulip, with the tendency to bend, head lowered to the ground and never attempting to contort itself into the elegant dance of a lily, or the bite of a proudly flirtatious orchid. The 'weeds' happily flowering and thriving have no idea that we have labelled them such.

It strikes me how much we could learn by following their example, to be as we were intended to be, true to ourselves. We all come here with an Earthly purpose, equipped with skills, and our own truth is only derived when we embrace with open arms our ins and outs and our personal uniqueness. If nature intended us to be a sunflower, then we should hold our weighty, colourful head lofty and face the sunshine to the best of our ability. How many of us struggle to come to terms with our introverted tendencies amidst a group of extroverts, trying to rationalise our fear of the spotlight and vice versa; if only we emulated the plants and animals around us instead. I don't suppose it has ever crossed Travis's mind that his Jack Russell dog life would be more complete if only he had the luxuriant, swinging coat of the Afghan Hound or the statuesque poise of the Great Dane. I wonder how bad things ever occur on Earth, when such simple marvels as these tiny plants can be found in dark, neglected corners. At times I've felt it isn't the roses that we need to stop and smell, since they have their own way of flaunting their voluptuous, elegance and have already found their beloved place in society. It's the unsung tiny heroes that we should perhaps take the moments to salute.

❊

As a mark of respect for this wonderful plant-optimism and for the defiance these tiny giants exhibit, I paint. I paint blooms and leaves, in a dynamic and colourful way that grants them longevity and a voice that I feel they rightly deserve. More often it is the special leaf, curled up on the grass and in its dying throws of colour and form that takes me in and warms my heart. If the timing is right and one's eyes are lucky enough to rest on such a leaf mid-sunbeam, the spectacle is truly a gift, an autumnal palette of amber, copper, burgundy and lime and a reminder that this little leaf is part of the much bigger picture and an almost magical connection. I am always profoundly touched by such tiny fragments and reminded of the constant and reassuring cycle of nature. No matter what transpires, nature can be relied upon. Buds will sprout into succulent leaves until it is time for them to adopt autumn's striking hues and finally be shed, in preparation for another season to begin. And so it is.

I will spend weeks, months even, carving a blank canvas with my paint-soaked brushes, until I feel I've given that little leaf the respect it deserves. I lean towards depicting my subjects against a dark background of moody and atmospheric tones. It strikes me that this is the best way to capture the essence of an emerging bloom or leaf as it bursts forth from the canvas with all the energy it can muster. In this way, I paint to reflect life and how we should see the darkness as our ally and friend instead of the enemy within. It is out of the darkness that we can measure our own strengths and only from that muted backdrop can we see the contrast of light and hope and love. The sludge-green, spinach-soup-of-life, clearly enhances for us the brilliance of a kaleidoscope of infinite colour around us and we can appreciate and be thankful for every single tone.

I am forever grateful to nature for bestowing on us these wonders. The sad days would be much sadder deplete of Mother Nature and the more we stop to look at the gems around us, the more happiness takes over and joy snuggles in. The world and all its glory finally begins to make some sense.

So I was looking forward to Gabon, to a jungle home and being in nature's hands for a few years and feeling blessed at the prospect of having the opportunity to capture some of that spirit on canvas. I was full of expectation too that somehow in this back-to-nature nothingness, something in me would stir back into blossoming life after too many years of lacklustre and, a bit like the autumn leaves, feeling curled up emotionally. I'd grown tired of living shut-down and of living with my light dimmed. It seemed to me the jungle would be the perfect place to turn my own head fully to the sun, to soak in the healing rays and to rejoice at having survived the storm clouds of the last few years. I felt I was open to making the changes that were necessary to achieve this. I knew that living my truth was somehow vital to me.

After a reasonably uneventful flight, senses perhaps numbed by a combination of fatigue and fear, we touched down in Gabon. In an over-hot Arrivals hall, we encountered a tedious wait in what could only be loosely described as a queue. It was a queue in the same sense that sand waits in a queue to pass from one bulbous compartment to the other in an egg-timer. I was surprised and disappointed in myself for not having anticipated this exhausting arrival scenario considering we'd previously had five years of a similar airport experience in Nigeria. I felt more than a few bubbles of anxiety rising and a vulnerability that I wished would settle. Eventually we reached the Customs desk, quickly found enough French words for required responses to the officials, showed evidence of our compulsory Yellow Fever inoculations and hurried to the luggage hall to look for Travis.

Remarkably, he appeared to have coped well with the trauma of being transported alongside luggage and in a windowless cabin, a far cry from his preferred automobile seating. Travis has become accustomed to travelling in style, straddling the back and front car seats with his paws balanced on the little centre console and eyes focused on the road ahead as he surfs the corners, remaining perfectly balanced at all times. He has the balancing skill of a champion of water sports. To the onlooker he could easily be confused as some car mascot, proudly placed inside the car instead of being cast in chrome and banished to suffer the elements on the bonnet.

He only seemed mildly perturbed now to be circling a luggage conveyor belt in Africa, in his transit cage with his little grey water dish, the best value excess baggage we've ever paid for.

As swiftly as possible, negotiating the crowds of travellers queuing alongside us, apprehensively waiting to exit Customs with their duty free status intact, we left the airport, luggage accounted for, and boarded the company bus. International travel evidently suited our canine travelling companion well and he made it his business to socialise with people who wanted to be sociable and did his best to try to win round the ones who didn't. He was a welcome distraction from our own exhausted thoughts, buzzing along with the mosquitoes around our heads. The feeling was that our journey was nearly over and simultaneously just beginning.

We had to stay overnight in the capital city Libreville before taking the flight to the camp the next day. The hotel was adequate if lacking in brightness, coolness and modern touches and morning arrived after comfortable enough but certainly not refreshing sleep. My husband and I tried our best to remain excited by the newness of the unfolding events and after a bus ride to the airstrip we boarded the `plane headed for the camp. The small `plane with its maximum 50-person capacity was so over-laden with luggage that we had all been instructed to give each individual piece of baggage a priority rating. The balance would hopefully be flown down the next day, or the day after that. This was Africa after all and one needed to allow some margins. Once the small `plane was airborne, we flew over lagoon after lagoon, each peppered by tiny islands of forest, floating like sort of miniature trees that could be painstakingly stuck on a painted board by an enthusiast for a model train to chuff past. After seemingly miles and miles of lagoon and indications of the remoteness ahead, a flight time of around an hour and a half and plenty of time to ponder the enormity of being deposited into a camp of people that we'd never met before, like new fish being emptied into an already balanced aquarium, we began the descent. As seasoned expatriates, we were only too aware of the upsets our arrival might bring to the equilibrium of the settled microcosm.

I often wonder what goes through the minds of travellers gazing out of aeroplane windows, some on sad missions, communing to weep, some destined for romantic liaisons and some losing their thoughts with every passing cloud, calm and de-tuned from the grind of their daily routines. I too had been drinking in the view, the beauty of Africa and wondering how life would be. Would old wounds be stirred to rawness once more or healed and integrated like knots on the trunks of ancient trees, almost concealing any evidence of past traumas as they blend into and even enhance the deepening patina?

Chapter 2

Shedding Branches

To say that Africa is a great teacher is not an understatement; lessons are learned every day. The place has a way of opening you up raw. It's almost as if with every turn you come face to face with a mirrored version of yourself reflecting back your imperfections and the disquiet of your very soul. It didn't take many weeks for me to feel the effects of such a major life-disruption. I could only compare myself to a great oak whose branches all fell off in one almighty crack and came crashing down, shockingly, to the ground. I reasoned, amidst the trauma, that the only way up would be to grow new ones to replace the empty feeling that overwhelmed me. I also reasoned that it was a time to be patient, not one of my strengths. It was likely, anyway, that I'd been carrying around a bundle of branches that didn't serve a useful purpose and had been limiting my progress. I knew that. I could see that my earlier sentiments were already manifesting and, despite previous African camp life experience in Nigeria, this country and the remoteness of our bizarre little housing estate would prove to be a life-changing thing. There was nothing more to do than to get on with the job in hand. At least my trunk felt intact and my roots felt strongly embedded into Mother Earth and I was sure this was a good sign.

The camp is nestled inbetween jungle areas and appears as a strangely cultivated oasis amidst lush but undeveloped surroundings. There are some 140 houses, from three-bedroom compact bungalows to one-bedroom studios, most in tired condition with maintenance being restricted both by a lack of urgency and by available materials. We've a 'Management Row', skirting the lake with large, splendid managerial patios offering up some of the best views on the camp. The bonus of the higher standard of accommodation is tempered somewhat, however, by the knowledge that these houses have been built on a former graveyard. Across the road from number 12, a strange red letterbox (alarmingly misplaced due to the lack of any mail service here) is for depositing notes containing messages for the deceased buried under the houses there. The rest of the houses are placed randomly, and almost appear to have taken up their precise locations after being numbered and scattered like handfuls of dice. Number 32 is directly next to 88, while 60 has 112 as a neighbour and so on. Explanations for the illogical and confusing numbering system indicate that the houses were numbered in the order in which they were built. Most houses these days have patios guarded with plastic mosquito net - a company safety response to the death of a resident some years ago - from the constant background threat of malaria here.

Gardens are somewhat undefined and unbounded and efforts to grow flowers in the sandy soil, along with any of the vegetation on the camp providing a source of elephant gastronomy, deter many from investing too much energy in the gardening department. There is a liberal sprinkling of the most spectacular, towering bamboo plants growing around the place and it seems that every second tree is an elephant-attracting mango. A few large rubber plants sprout exotically here and there, having slipped through the company's elimination programme. Rubber plants are incredibly attractive to snakes apparently and flout company health and safety parameters. (The eucalyptus of Oman and its extreme liking for a drink in a water-challenged desert country had also been banned from cultivation there.)

Some Yenzi camp residents try to bolster the lack of vegetables available by growing such things as herbs and tomatoes. If they are lucky, they will be harvested and chopped up ripe in a salad bowl, set off with a glistening dressing and some shavings of parmesan cheese, painstakingly purchased and carried out to Gabon from a supermarket at home. It's more than likely though that the tomatoes will be entrapped prematurely in an elephant's trunk before being thrown backwards into a gaping and receptive mouth. Elephants don't have a palate for basil or chilli plants apparently, so these are sometimes used as a protection for guarding more delicious crops concealed inbetween these undesired stems. But elephants are clever animals it seems and understand that a rummage in almost anything can yield gastronomic delights. Such is the elephant's tendency to rummage that the company's Safety Department has gone to the length of constructing metal cages at the foot of the driveway of every house to ensure the dustbins are sited a lofty three feet off the ground. This attempt at keeping menacing elephant trunks out of dustbins has only minimal success and there is daily evidence of discarded bin lids and rubbish strewn at the foot of many driveways. My little basil plant in its tomato tin, exempt from the elephants' preferred eating list appeared, unfortunately, to be a delicacy to ants and provided evidence of the fight for survival and delicate balance of such rainforest environments. Slowly I was learning to appreciate some of rudiments of this particular jungle habitat.

We have low-level street lighting on Yenzi Camp and most residents tend to keep exterior illumination to respectable jungle levels. Lights burning for any time here attract bugs, like bees to honey or housewives to the camp store as soon as word circulates that the weekly food shipment has arrived on camp, flown in from Libreville.

On one frightening occasion, I'd left our outside area and car port lights shining brightly, in a similar manner to a High Street decked with rows of festive lights months ahead of Christmas. On this evening there hadn't been a single light bulb that I'd neglected to engage in the task of illumination. I learned to my cost that in this location this is a most risky procedure. I'd erroneously thought that a darkened car port, fooled into daylight by two spotlights, two florescent tubes and miscellaneous other bulbs beaming brightly into the African night, would send snakes scurrying into the dark and away. I'd omitted to take into account the habit bugs have for banging their heads into shining lights and this night I ran screaming hysterically from our kitchen door into our car for safety. The car, white and glowingly luminously bright, was sending out a plethora of bug party invitations and whilst I sat in the driver's seat, shaking my hair to empty it of wildlife, I noticed the bonnet by now was like an entomologist's lifetime's bug collection, only still crawling, buzzing and flapping simultaneously. One in particular caught my eye. He sat hunched up and large, like a small frog beside the windscreen wipers, terrifying even through glass. Others scampered over the windows, big, small, bright and colourful or unassuming. I eventually summoned up the courage to drive off in the direction of the social club some two minutes away, undertaking the sharpest corners that I felt the cumbersome four-wheel drive would permit me make without landing on its side. Only when I was certain that the creatures would by now have released their grip of the car bodywork would I attempt to exit the vehicle. I returned home later that night to find that a break-away bug party had also formed inside our house. On entering the kitchen I was unnerved to witness butterflies, moths and their winged cousins partaking in a synchronised air show, whilst those more adept on the ground were negotiating the worktops. Horrified by the scene, I promised myself to learn to adapt to the darkness. They say that yellow bulbs, with their sickly jaundiced-glow that makes the houses look centuries older than their forty years, have less appeal to the bug world. At that level bugs and humans appear to be united.

Our house follows the property mantra of location, location, location, but the occupants in houses in the centre of the camp have windows that I envy every time I walked past. For some strange reason, we seem to be lacking in glass and light in our little home and, from a seated position, it's almost impossible to see anything outside except the tops of exotic, swaying palm branches in the distance laden with squawking African Grey parrots eating the jewel-like red palm fruits. In addition, the small windows we do have are tinted shades darker than the average pair of sunglasses and it always surprises me in the morning to find the outside sky offering up a more beautiful blue or lighter grey than might first be deduced by looking out of our windows. Evidently, the spinach paint will need good lighting to enable us to see anything inside clearly at all.

I have no doubt that any reputable interior designer would be doing their level best to coax us to a more light-reflecting paint choice than the spinach soup on its way to us but we will not be moved. To make such a dramatic decoration change, after months of fantasising about the end result, would be to wave the white flag of surrender and to place our entire life, lock stock and barrel in the hands of the institutionalised company. If we were to make that concession, we might as well don company overalls and become peas in a pod. No. Whatever the lighting challenge, the dark green walls and individuality would prevail. In any case, if memory served we had several functional head torches coming in our freight, to serve as a Plan D if all else struggled to illuminate.

We are located on Monkey Road, named for the monkeys that occupy the jungle that wraps around our little cul-de-sac. They are a treat to watch and with our small patio directly facing one of their favoured jungle areas, our house has a definite desirability element. As well as the monkeys, from the relative privacy of the patio it is possible to take in the sights outside almost undetected, watching other members of the camp going about their business.

In a camp of limited store cupboard food options, the little Club boulangerie with its fresh daily croissants, patisseries and baguettes can raise the spirits, in ways that such calorific and carbohydrate-ridden feasts would raise eyebrows in abundant and health-conscious Europe. A common sight around the camp are locals, housemaids (or ménagères as they are known in Gabon) and foreigners alike, walking or cycling, laden with their daily stash of unwieldy baguettes. My first few attempts at safely transporting the ten-minute walk home such lengthy bread, still perfectly erect and not drooped in half, were alarmingly fraught. As if to reinforce the point that you had arrived at 'ground zero' and the foot of the newcomers' learning curve, even the skill of carrying a loaf of bread home was beset with challenges and needed a hefty application of local knowledge. On each occasion when I tried to carry my shopping home, within minutes of embarking on the homeward walk my bread would be perilously close to bowing its head so low that it was touch and go if I'd make it back to safety before it snapped in half, depositing a healthy lunch time sandwich length on the ground. I also struggled with the notion that, when transported in the customary small, inferior plastic bags more appropriate to carry a single 'pain au chocolate', the bread, with its anatomical dough end protruding into the air, looked farcically rude and somewhat phallic to carry at such an early hour and in a camp buzzing with young children. In some senses, I took relief from its decision to bend more modestly, relaxing from its upright pose. Attempting to carry several baguettes at a time required intermittent tweaking of the individual droops, in much the same ways as an entertainer might spin plates perched on long wires, giving each enough fair attention to remain intact until the safety of home and the worktop was reached.

My first forays of leaping down our garden, mimicking our monkey neighbours and their strange bird-like calls, were met with limited success in that on each occasion this unsubtle approach had the poor things running for cover and me standing more red-faced than their red-topped heads. They are fascinating to watch and uncannily child-like as they stuff fruits into their mouths, with a look that shouts out "You can't catch me, ha-ha". Needless to say, Travis has new sights on his horizon and we have a new and unusual training problem on our hands, probably not covered in any chapter of our Jack Russell training manual.

Monkey Lane, coursing along the bottom of our garden, turns into Lizard Lane somewhere around Pompier Corner, where our fire crew and single splendid fire engine are reassuringly staked out. As with its counterpart, it gets its name from the two-metre Monitor lizards that have made this area of the camp their own residential estate. Monitors, though not deadly, can be aggressive and inflict a painful bite even through a sturdy safety boot and should be observed from a safe distance. Over-confident pet dogs have been known to be whipped in the face by the lashing tails of angry Monitors unappreciative of persistent canine invitations to play.

It didn't take long to work out that this sort of close proximity living had a tendency to make some of our camp neighbours withdraw, to the extent that they might as well have fitted shutters to their heads or make-shift hedges to protect them from external onslaught. There was a look of sheer terror spread across their faces as we newcomers tried to elicit a conversation, constructing sentences and an exchange. They were only comfortable parting with a distant "How are you?", the response often falling on their vanishing heels. It was evident that they had no energy reserves for such chat and possible that life in this location could at times be so consuming that what little reserves were left had to be given away in carefully measured doses. Once unpacked and settled and far removed from the newcomers' list, one didn't want to be dragged back down answering beginners' questions. Existence in places such as this can be so fragile and draining that, once you have fought for acceptance, you don't want to rock any boats that might have you slipping back down the curve. I often think that in hardship locations, like Gabon and Nigeria, survival and coping feels a lot like pedalling a bike up a steep hill. If wheels aren't motored forwards each day, slowly and surely, then you find yourself crashing into the blues at the bottom of the hill, scratching your head and nursing your wounds and wondering what went wrong. Complacency can be the scourge of tough locations.

Of course, there were exceptions to this cool behaviour, whose kindness and keenness to befriend strangers was remarkable and touching. At times though, camp life was like being cast in some strange psychological movie or cult film. My days would begin brimming with optimism and before I'd even reached lunchtime my spirit would be drained by this strange phenomenon. It was the last thing I'd expected to find and it made me angry. I promised myself to keep buoyant and not be dragged down, and headed out each morning on my dog walks soaking in all the jungle air, gradually becoming less afraid of the notion of some creature running out to grab, sting or bite me with every day that passed.

I'm a chicken when it comes to creatures, especially of the insect variety, having run away from my own hair tickling my face whilst living in the UK. In a tropical creature pot like this, my senses were on the highest alert. There's probably a very good reason; I was born as a Scot, in Edinburgh, a climate where only the most die-hard beasties fly through the sky with teeth. I don't recall ever being on guard in case a python slithered out to snatch me or my hairy companions, whilst doing my turn walking the family dogs as a child. I did once have a painful stinging episode from a wasp that I'd unwittingly sat on. On climbing aboard my tricycle I'd failed to see the additional black spot that had settled in alongside the three regular black screws that kept my little yellow saddle in place. I still remember the moment of pain and the application of after-sting on my behind, in front of a family that could barely conceal its amusement. To this day, I'm not sure if it was the wasp or the humiliation that hurt the most. If I'd been in the audience perhaps I'd have been stifling a laugh or two as well, but on the receiving end their attention felt far from that of compassion.

❉

As the jungle days ticked by I couldn't help thinking that I'd arrived in Africa as a balloon, full of air that was slowly gasp by gasp leaking out. I was sure my ebb of energy was visible to all who observed my dog walks. I was now well aware of my shoulders slouching and a deflation in my stride. Even Travis was exhibiting signs of his own unhappiness, or possibly depression, as he slumped in his little bed and had to be coaxed, often unsuccessfully, to go for 'walkies'. I was glad we'd made his bed one of the high-priority packing items and that it had so brilliantly fitted into one of the golf bags, even also serving to keep the golf balls warm in transit. At least he was miserable in a familiar bed. I knew well by now the wretched feeling of making do in a tired and uncomfortable, loan-float double bed. Our company bed is visibly banana-shaped and creaks like an ancient castle door easing itself reluctantly open when you climb into it. The luxury of winding the day up, and retreating to bed to renew and refresh, is tainted by this groaning monstrosity and by the discomfort of having your spine curve unnaturally to follow its aged lines.

I was not alone in my sentiments; my husband was suffering his own beginner's low, missing the comfort of familiar things, exacerbated by this diffused 'welcome' we'd arrived to. At least we had a common interest and a united problem. With all negatives, there is always light to be found in the darkness. A silver lining and a glimmer of a bud that could spring into colourful glory.

I knew my personal low would pass and over the years have learned what I need to do to lift the clouds when the sky feels as though it is pressing heavily on my shoulders. I take as much time out as I need, retreating into my virtual cave and ponder. I meditate and I release some of the emotional turmoil in my painting. I grumble a bit, listen to music and listen to silence. I'd packed some small blank canvases in my suitcase, at the expense of unnecessary luxury items like wooden spoons and a rolling pin. Given the deficits in the kitchen department, I'd surprisingly managed to roll out home-made pizza bases, estimating quantities with the absence

of scales and measuring spoons, and flattened resistant dough by imple-
menting the use of a roll of cling film. Times spent alone with my paints
and brushes, taking in glimpses of trees outside and the cacophony of the
nature chants, felt self-contained and blissfully removed from this unfriendly mood outside. It's a good thing that moments are all temporary,
from the highest high to the lowest low, and just like the movement of the
hands on the ticking clock even the testing times are thankfully never
frozen still. I always try to remind myself of this fact, when I check-in to my
solitude.

I knew, with a certainty, that my air would fill up again and lightness
would replace my heavy limbs and heart. Even a spiritual warrior, tripped
up from time to time, needs to re-group thoughts and deadhead negative
behavioural patterns. It is always a matter of time and perspective, of
tuning more into the details around and into nature to restore personal
harmony and balance to whatever might be out of kilter. It seems to be that
the more attention is paid to the tiniest of details, the bigger and more
marvellous the picture becomes and the less one notices life's buzzes and
blips. They are only, after all, a distracting façade from the peace that
resides deep within each of us and which we too often fail to notice.

Very slowly I began to relax into the camp environs, mesmerised by the
birdsong and the greenness around me that I now realised I'd been missing
after many years of living in the Middle East. African Grey parrots flew in
friendly flocks over the camp with their distinctive cut-off beaks and flashy
red tails, madly flapping and inelegant, as though they might not make it to
the safety of the next branch. Occasionally, from our patio the place would
be like an orchestra of nature: birds, parrots and monkeys, all fluttering,
jumping and chirping to some imaginary conductor's directions. I was
warming, lifting and beginning to bounce back, as I knew I would.

Chapter 3

King Herod Needs to be Rescued

I'd had a sticky few years, somehow finding myself stumbling and tripping along a winding path that appeared to offer little in the way of respite and instead threw up unending bumps. It seemed that no matter how carefully I stepped, I was always choosing the toughest route and advancing slowly. At times I felt like I was making no progress at all, like running around the foot of the mountain but never able to advance up its slopes. The family had had a posting upset and were now dealing with deep emotional fallout and for me there was the sense of life coming unhinged in such a way that it felt as though mind, body and soul had been squeezed simultaneously through a mangle.

As a result of this, the relationship between my husband and I had become strained and we'd reached somewhat of a parting of emotional paths. Events had conspired to fracture what we'd always assumed was a solid, unbreakable union. Icy chasms had now widened so large that it was impossible even to jump to safety over them. Maybe we just drifted off course, got distracted and stopped seeing each other's best sides. A travelling life, moving frequently as we had for so many years, comes with advantages and certain disadvantages and life's normal blips can feel particularly amplified and destructive in insular locations. There is the challenge to adapt to the new environment and to build a life making the best of the resources available, and a satisfaction that comes from seeing your own progress, mapped out by every new road navigated and every new hand shaken, until you have earned the right to be removed from the newcomers' list. Exotic lives can and do generate stress, a different kind of stress from home, that seems at loggerheads with palm trees and sun tan lotion. Couples often drift apart through too many extended periods of enforced separation as mothers make the frequent and lengthy trips back to base country to spend time re-bonding with their boarding school children. Long-term partners can lose appeal in the midst of the foreign excitement of some exotic locations. The old and familiar, the comfortable shoes, functional but uninspiring, appear dull and mundane amidst the technicoloured buzz of some places and couples frequently pull apart. To an extent we'd fallen victims to the curse of this expat life. The high risk to married life was something we were all too aware of. It was hard at times for wives to be able to live to their fullest potential in many of the more difficult locations and if delivering up the finest scones and stews for your friends from a dismal selection of ingredients available wasn't the thing that simultaneously fed you at soul level, discontent would seed and grow to a choking forest. Even in the days before the expansion of online networking, there was usually efficient circulation of the latest spouse-separation details that did the rounds in these living microcosms. The skills honed from the years of ladies' tennis mornings were utilised to ensure that the relevant juicy details were sent like sharply executed volleys from one ear to the next at lightning speed.

As far as our home life is concerned, there are no insults hurled crashing against the walls and somehow we maintain a level of friendship, united enough to keep the outside world happy, silently shedding our internal tears. Life is calm enough. Underneath, we both mourn the loss of closeness and essential respect for one another that forms a base of a great relationship. Sometimes I feel I carry the sadness like a shell on my back, laden down by the feeling of lack, of living at only 70% of my loving capacity. I believe this is where my empathy for my little step flowers stems from. When I stop to admire their resilience, I see something of myself smiling back, small but sincere and trying to live from the heart. A survivor. We should never be judged for our lack of obvious luxuriant, colourful petals and swinging stem. Beauty doesn't always need to shout in fruity, operatic tones from the rooftops, but can hum quietly its own gentle, almost inaudible melody. I'm not entirely sure of my husband's feelings, since we keep our painful thoughts to ourselves and act out our public charade of togetherness.

❈

To an extent, we are to marriages what kitten heels are to the world of fashion, on the mediocre side of the scale. I've always loathed kitten heels that try to tread carefully along the line between the yelling sexiness of a full-on high-heeled stiletto and the mundane practicality of a loafer. I'm even more infuriated when they dress themselves up in risqué animal guise and provocative leather shimmer. At a moment's glimpse they may fool, but all intrigue is lost the minute that dreaded Lilliputian heel exposes itself. I don't care that bunions may form in later life and backs may break from years of trotting around perched on decadent heels. Surely if the heels don't get you, the handbag will anyway and it seems sensible to spread the risk. I detest the wishy-washiness of these kittens, the daring to put the toe in the water, but never the foot and Heaven forbid the knee. I'm all for passion, when something lights you up so much that every cell in your body is talking the same talk at the same time. A buzz. Be it approval or disapproval, there should be no middle ground, not of marriages and not of shoes and certainly not of life. Mid-range is so average.

❈

Gabon and our jungle living could have been a cleansing, a new slate and fresh start, a time to prune the deadwood and facilitate a new, healthy relationship and growth; but each of us, focused on our own sense of injustice, so far hasn't been able to take the first step. In the meantime we carry on with our own voyages of discovery, of self-discovery and test ourselves, rip ourselves apart in this new, raw country and begin to build ourselves back again, to be reborn, bushy and vibrant with a renewed certainty in who we are and our place in the world.

❈

Several years back, when life fell off its predicted rails, I hadn't know where to turn, nor whom to turn to on my search for peace, and at the time didn't consider for one minute that peace was already there for me to shake hands with if only I took the time and patience to find it and diverted my search within. I was too busy casting my eye to the sky for a miracle, for something or someone to fall down and rescue me from my misery. The last thing I considered was to look to myself for a resolution.

I'd decided to launch myself into a spiritual search, nudged on by my unhappiness. First on my list of things-to-do was to learn Reiki, whatever that was; I wasn't even sure I knew, only that it was of the greatest importance for me to acquire the skills. `Phone numbers were exchanged by friends of friends and it wasn't long before I found myself shaking hands and exchanging hugs with two of the calmest, kindest ladies I'd ever met. If this was the fruits of Reiki I couldn't wait to dine. At this point in my life, nests had been emptied by the wrench of our two boys, still young, departing from our house in Nigeria for boarding school. They'd settled well there and seemed to thrive, grasping the opportunity to plant their Scottish roots after years of warm and exotic living. It was my husband and I who bore the strain of it, the ultimate decision in the conveyor belt of this travelling life, and at loggerheads with all maternal and paternal nurturing instincts. I think much of our subsequent marital derailment was due to us not managing to reconcile this separation.

The two Reiki ladies lived together in a compact house nestled in a small village in the East Lothian countryside. I knocked on their door full of excitement, the sort of fluttering of the heart that one might get from entering a doctor's surgery for a prescription of a miracle tablet to erase all your problems and deliver you softly and swiftly on a one-way trip to Utopia. The walls of the house were full of art painted by one of the kind ladies, which I was later to learn was "emitting healing Reiki rays into the atmosphere". At the time that concept seemed somewhat alien to me, but many years down the line, I understand there can be no clear-cut separation of such natural creative gifts and inherent healing energy. A painting will always speak on a multi-dimensional level, stirring, warming, shocking or whatever, according to the message painted therein. There is so much more to behold from a paining than arrangement of colour and form taken at purely face value.

The small living room was darkened from the un-seasonally bright day by tightly-closed curtains and softly lit with lamps and plentiful sparkling candles, like shimmering stars, dotted around. I pushed the initial apprehension that rose on entering the sacred space out of my mind and took my seat on the sofa. There was a love and a calmness contained in the space that enfolded me and I felt instantly safe and secure. The ladies went to pains to explain to me the history and principles behind Reiki. I listened intently, fascinated also to learn that one of my lovely teachers had been struck down with a disabling disease several years ago and through tapping into this healing energy was not only mobile but agile, despite a medical prognosis that would have had her in a wheelchair long before now. The ladies also worked their calming magic on animals and regularly had dog residents checked in for a few weeks at a time. On this occasion, a slumbering black Labrador by the name of Soot, lay in the kitchen unfazed by strange visitors and doorbells and seemed to be a good advertisement for the ability of this Reiki to bring serenity.

Reiki is an ancient Japanese technique for stress-reduction and relaxation that also promotes healing. It is administered by a 'laying-on of hands' and is based on the idea that unseen energy flows through the practitioner to the client. If our energy field is low, then we are more likely to get sick or feel stress; and if it is high, we are more capable of being happy and healthy. Reiki can be used to heal physical bodies, emotions, events and situations past and present, and it seemed just the prescription I needed. In order to be able to self-heal it was necessary to go through some little ritualised ceremonies, performed by the Reiki Master and chief of the kind ladies. I sat upright in a chair, palms together in prayer position, while she moved quietly about me, occasionally chanting beneath her breath or tapping me on the shoulders. My ladies informed me that the room was full of angels and their eyes would dart here and there, following the angelic sightings. It struck me as a bizarre thing to be happening in a community of such huddled together houses and I was sure that neighbourly blinds and curtains must twitch, trying to work out the untimely closure of window drapes and arrivals of strange guests such as myself. I had unwavering belief in my teachers' angelic reports and a renewed faith that life would work out for the best, given time - perhaps a lot of time.

I headed off back into the world with a comfort blanket and a growing suspicion that there was more to this life than meets the eye. I was determined that my woes would not be the things that defined me and that some day I would indeed see them as my blessings and springboard into a new way of thinking and of being. We are never alone and nothing happens by chance; even in the throes of the lowest low your angels will be trying to get your attentions to help you. Only time would reveal my lesson, but whatever it was I knew that I was being nudged forwards through encountered pains in order to delve deeper into myself.

I Reiki-ed everything, trying to remember to 'order' ahead a parking place if I knew I was going to be driving to town, which was most often delivered as a perfectly convenient spot to rest my four wheels in. I sent healing to my children and husband and friends and family, a process involving placing my hands on a cushion and allowing the healing energy to flow to the parts of my distant patient that required it. Sometimes, it's best not to wonder too much about the how and why these things work, but merely to have faith that they do. The feedback I would get during these treatments would be tingling and, often, incredible warmth in my hands when I was focusing on an area that appeared to be in need of healing rays. I was stunned to be able to pick up and detect blockages in people separated from me by seas, continents and time.

I needed a spiritual comfort blanket to wrap around me during this bleak time, now finding myself living alone in Scotland, whilst my husband and children did their own work and school things. It was a tough time and the rudest of awakenings. Worst of all, nobody could see my torture, assuming wrongly that life in civilization must be a pleasure for me after five years of life in Third World Nigeria and the shock of a recent transatlantic evacuation. (I refer to it like that at this stage, rather than giving it the honour of being an actual country or specific location, so bad are the memories generated by that ghastly period.)

There is something incredibly humbling about living in such a demanding country as Nigeria, something that reminds you of your own fortunate life and of the blessings you have forgotten to see. Now that I was back in this European 'civilization' and world of abundance, it seemed that we were all too busy being busy to outstretch a hand of friendship, or too reserved to try to help mend a broken wing. I missed my former life, strangely lost without the confines of the friendly, barbed wire camp and its inhabitants and was struggling now to find my feet and regain a sense of purpose. It hit me like a thunderbolt that my being occupied in Nigeria and the skills gathered there were useless to me now and I envied the check-out girls at the supermarket for their ability to make a worthwhile living. I on the other hand had suspended my potential for years of fun and occasional tears, but felt I had nothing to show for it. It was as though I'd gorged on a chocolate box of exquisite tastes, but had been left with no real nutrition to equip me for life. I understood now what the term 'Trailing Spouse', as we are officially labelled, meant and wondered if the powers-that-be from the company who'd coined the term had intended the ridicule the name implied.

At this low time, being in the family home in Scotland, beautiful in a bijoux way and set in the middle of a little woodland, I was wracked with the thoughts of the boys being an hour away from me at boarding school and settled with their new school family and I felt my motherly role completely obsolete. I considered the high price of our travelling life, with the palm trees and the sundowners a lifetime away from me here in my Scottish weather-beaten woodland. In my many hours of solitude, my thoughts would go back over our Nigerian life and I wondered if we shouldn't have fought harder to keep our family intact and tried to relocate to a European country with provision for senior school education. Instead, one by one our lovely boys, barely into double figures, packed their cases and left Nigeria, bound for boarding school deep in the rolling Perthshire countryside.

The boys had made the most of Nigerian camp living and had voiced few complaints about the lack of child numbers they'd encountered on the camp. It concerned my husband and I most of all that suddenly they had been plucked from their thriving classes of more than twenty pupils and double streams in the previous post of Muscat, to a small school whose entire pupil complement would have fitted into a mere two classes. As with many things in Nigeria, they had to learn to compromise and to be grateful for the blessings a small cosy location offered. They were thankful to be part of a fun-filled community, welcomed at many events and along with us began to get a new perspective on their own good fortune. To this day, they are humbled by the sights that they witnessed in Nigeria and a poverty that they had only read of previously in story books, softened by pastel shaded colour sketches and always with a happy ending.

The school played its part in making up for a period of childhood that pretty much was played out behind the security - and limitations - of the camp's five kilometre barbed wire fence. There were school trips to exotic islands just off the equator and reached by special use of one of the company's Dornier `planes. These `planes had become a regular experience for us, delivering us and our heavy suitcases from Lagos and the international airport to our camp in Port Harcourt. The journey was always fraught, with back-to-back early morning flights and regular concerns as to whether the small Dornier would fly as scheduled. Very often the `plane would have been seconded to the company headquarters, full of VIP company personnel, whilst we were left to wait in a single room airport with the handful of warmed canned drinks and a sum total of a couple of apples available to us to while away the hours. On occasions this delay would have us stuck in that tiny room for hours at a time, faded and in need of something substantial to eat. The Nigerian Harmattan season is known as the period of time in the year when dust clouds blow down from the Sahara and the sky would be shaded and fogged by particles of suspended dust held in the winds. These loaded skies would at times cause all sorts of nasal congestion problems and all too frequently were the culprit for keeping our journey animatedly suspended in this frustrating way. The thick Harmattan could descend and blanket the place in diffused vision for hours or even days on end and make safe flying an impossibility. Most of us who regularly made the trips out of the Nigerian camp and back were used to spending inordinate amounts of time in this small airport departure room.

❋

In Nigeria, there were constant plays and nativity events organized on the Rumukoroshe camp and plenty of excitement to keep growing children happily stimulated. I remember one such amateur dramatic occasion when a bathroom door took it upon itself to malfunction at the most inopportune moment. Our youngest, who'd secured himself a respectable part in the production of a play, had inadvertently become stuck in our bathroom minutes before he should have been stepping into costume, a flowing purple gown and splendid crown adorned with macaroni jewels and sprayed to a majestic, glistening gold.

We didn't appreciate the severity of the situation until several smashing and freeing attempts had failed miserably and our little actor was no longer able to squeeze his tears back. Gulps began to gather momentum from behind the unco-operative door. The situation was now reaching emergency status and our eldest was dispatched to the school to inform anyone he could that King Herod was unavoidably delayed in the loo, but would surely be there soon.

My husband, now fuelled by little regal tears turning into gulps of hyperventilation from within the bathroom confines, decide to make runs at the door from the cooker in the kitchen, along the hallway with its lino tiles, to deliver a hefty kick to the stuck door. To add weight to the procedure he'd fastened an industrial protection boot to his right foot, hastily secured by a double knot for good measure. To our greatest amazement the door was refusing to yield its captive and was obviously better constructed than we'd given it credit for. Finally, as the greasepaint fumes were filling the school assembly hall and parents were taking to their seats, loaded with video cameras and sound equipment that the BBC would have envied, our little King was free. In the end it was going to be my husband's leg or the door that gave way and we were grateful that, in the end, human flesh had reigned supreme. We'd managed to bend the door and fractured its spine enough to pull little arms, now wet with tears, out. Without further ado King Herod was whisked into a waiting car and to the stage.

✾

Nigeria had been a challenge that we'd made the best of. We were a close and somewhat crazy community all brought together for overlapping years to laugh, cry and support each other in a place that you couldn't begin to describe to the folks back home. There were no words to convey the depths of the harrowing sights and sounds, nor the highs of managing to pull off any simple victory in such a place. I immersed myself in tennis lessons and became addicted to the humiliations of golf, playing regularly on the nine-hole course that was encased, as we were, within a barbed wire hedge.

The camp was full of colourful characters each playing their part, staying within their own boundaries and leaving specialist roles to those with the relevant mastery. Hating the limelight, I'd carved myself one of the creative roles, painting scenery for the plays, pantomimes and events that regularly filled the social calendar. The job suited me well and I relished the chance of a creative outlet, confident in my field and only mildly in awe of those who took to the actual stage and performed. It didn't really matter what part you played. This wasn't the forum for competition and we all knew that. What mattered was that we were each enhancing the other, a mutual exchange and fusion of talents. My scenery, painted on flat wooden boards, came to life when erected and lit by the lighting team and sprung into exciting animation when the costumed actors stepped into character, all amplified by the 'sound boys' in their technical den. This was teamwork at its best and I loved it.

Regularly, we were given an empty house on the camp for a few weeks, pre-renovation for its next occupants, to transform into a party house hosting the one or two key events in the social calendar. One year we worked for eight weeks, painting, sawing and constructing an Arabian themed party, for an International Night. My job was to help transform a tropical jungle garden into a desert for the evening and I worked with a team day in and day out, painting plywood boards each 4 ft by 8 ft with scenery. In the end we had more than sixty painted sections that pieced together, with windows and castellation painstakingly jig-sawn out by men keen to find a use for their over-specified tool boxes bulging with shiny, underused equipment. Ancient walls were carved from plywood to erect in sequence. The jungle garden was now masked behind a huge painted fortress façade and entered via ancient, brass-studded doors. You had to pass through a Middle Eastern souk, draped with lines of folded fabrics and stalls selling fruit and crafts, to arrive at the party. Everyone played a part in the transformation and if art wasn't your thing there was a 42 ft stage, dressed as an oversized Aladdin's lamp and guarded by a train of 16 ft high camels, awaiting keen performers.

These events were always a success, the culmination of so much team spirit, weeks of production and exotic, locally-made fancy dress costumes especially themed for the event. It was as if the party lasted for months and not merely a few hours on one sole evening. There were also, importantly, food and beverage teams who managed to produce from an often challenging market a culinary array of international cuisine for the event.

In addition to the Arabian themed event, there had been the Hallowe'en evening, where wooden coffins, purchased locally, were propped up around the living room of an empty house and which were later donated to lucky (or unlucky) eager, local recipients. We'd had the Punk night, with music played from a stage bedecked in huge wooden boards cut and painted to resemble razor blades and a London Underground entrance, complete with buskers and a ticket desk, from which you were to receive your welcome drink. The ingenuity and creativity of such an eclectic mix of people never failed to impress me, along with the enormous energy people were prepared to expend to do their bit to contribute. Nigeria wasn't a place where you wanted too much spare time on your hands.

Once a year, we had the 'Playback' evenings, where my creative role would be the backstage production side and scene-setting, from which the more exhibitionist would mime in costume to their chosen songs. This was always one of my favourite evenings. We'd have Madonna and Robbie Williams strutting their stuff, and the Full Monty-type acts with wigs made from string mops bought at the local market. There were always the risqué acts towards the end of the evening that we could rely on to entertain us. A Spice Girl act was always a prerequisite. This would usually be a troupe of men in disguise, in their market-bought wigs, leopard thongs over tights and nipples honed by the careful snipping of pieces of sponge, placed with almost too much precision. It was ironic that after the weekend was over and the debris cleared up, these men would again be occupying their office seats and communicating in altogether more sober attire and at a more serious level.

✷

In our empty home in Scotland now, I longed for my friends and missed being a part of such a huge extended family and to be able to play my artistic part in themed productions, feeling too fragile now even to stand behind my own canvases, even though I knew that in the capacity of painter and when standing behind my canvases, I am at my nearest to wholeness. I needed my new spiritual blanket to warm me and to help me to try to make sense of a world that appeared to fall apart at times. An increasing awareness of the power and love of the universe was the only thing to give comfort and, crucially, something that could never be removed, extracted or fall through a chasm out of my reach. It was mine to have for infinity.

At this empty time, I also had the greatest support from a wonderful lady who would email me her assessment of the bigger picture she could see around me, when I was overly occupied in focusing on the painful fragments instead. Her wisdom and her intuitive gift was, at times, a vital life force to me and her loving support brought some welcome light to these dark moments. She remains a unique and special person to me, with a desire to see individuals rise to their fullest potential.

Nigeria had been a tough beginning in a harsh and often cruel environment. The first sights that met our eyes on arrival are forever burned into our memory: beggars, many limb-less, lepers and starving children, held in the embrace of severe poverty. The world that we'd left felt much more distant than a mere six hour long-haul flight away, with its complimentary champagne served by smiling, uniformed stewardesses and with the latest movie choice. It is beyond reason that human beings, by some strange geographical throw of the dice, could be dealt such a hard blow and be faced with such insurmountable struggles as this to contend with.

After lengthy delays and duties paid to Customs officials, we had left the relative safety of the Murtala Muhammed airport and had somehow managed to negotiate the mass hysteria that the arrival of us foreigners created. Shouts of 'Oyibos' echoed from all directions with varied intensity. Oyibos, or 'No Skins', we quickly discovered, was the term used to describe us pale-skinned expatriates. We forcibly pushed outstretched and grabbing hands away, attempting to coax ancient and partially wheel-less, heavily-laden luggage trolleys over potholes and to the safety of the company vehicle that we understood was to be waiting for us. The sight of one particular man, a leper with a disfigured face and eyeball missing, had particularly disturbed us all. It seemed for all the company formalities processed by various departments to get a family relocated from one country to another, not enough focus had been placed on really making us aware of the harrowing sights we would encounter, nor how to deal with the idea of meeting others so less fortunate than ourselves. Once in the security of the bus, curtained as a security measure to conceal the identity of the occupants and with an air-conditioner set to a brisk Scottish winter temperature, we breathed a collective sigh of horror-filled relief. Most of our thoughts at that moment were of sending CVs and job applications off to get us as quickly as possible out of the waking nightmare. Our children, aged six and eight, were visibly shaken by the ordeal of arriving in such an inhospitable place and we did our best to reassure them and offer our inadequate explanations for the horror movie that they appeared to have now been cast in.

Nigerian camp living, unlike the unbounded camp in the Middle East we'd previously known, was a caged facility, secured by razor-wire and security check-points. The houses themselves were protected by wrought iron grilles, padlocked over every window and door entry point. Even the interior and safe haven had prison-like metal doors to be locked by padlock at night on retiring to bed, to offer extra protection to the sleeping quarters. It had been said that one of the houses had had a stowaway living in the roof space, recognised as an easy point of entry due to a flimsy tin roof. Even now years later, I cannot think of Nigeria without the idea of great, clanking padlocks rattling in my head.

We'd inherited a complete staff contingent from the previous occupants of 4 Bomu Crescent, and even before we'd unpacked all eight of our over-stuffed suitcases it was evident we'd made a terrible mistake. The 'ironing-dusting girl' called Happiness, of all things, had to go - now! Her insolence was something I couldn't bear to have sharing my air-space and as she swung a duster over the filthy skirting boards, one hand resting cheekily on her hip and glaring menacingly at me, I served her notice. This left a cook, a driver and three gardeners remaining in our employ. It had been a mistake to go along with the suggestion of the previous occupants of the house to take on their huge staff contingent. It was something we were not used to and something we didn't want. There was the expectation that as overseas visitors we were obligated in some way to provide local employment but this was a level way beyond our comfort.

The cook Mercy, heavily pregnant and most times to be found seated, head in her arms rested on a little table in the centre of our kitchen, and the sister of Happiness the dusting girl, lasted barely two weeks. I still wince at her constant delight in shocking me with tales of how her former 'madam' was murdered some years ago on the camp whilst she was babysitting the family. I didn't want to know and wanted, like the other camp residents, to put the horror of that story out of my head. It would be hard enough to keep a positive momentum in this place, without detailed knowledge of such brutality.

Our house was in dire need of some TLC, as is the case in such a damp rain-soaked country. It seems as if nature has to be pushed back some inches from the doorstep every now and again and green mould scraped from greying walls. One has to stamp one's authority on arrival. Though limited in resources and challenged in others, there was no shortage of local workmen keen to bolster their salaries by taking on extra part-time work and in no time we had the place crawling with willing, if not always appropriately skilled, labourers. This was the sort of place where a tradesman sent from the company to make some of the frequently needed repairs to your house could try to repair a leaking tap with a few threads ripped from the edge of his shirt, or smooth grouting between tiles with his flip-flop.

There was so much to be done to our new house that the only sensible move was for the family to decamp to the largest bedroom, with its en-suite bathing facility. The four of us lived, eating and sleeping in one room and bathroom for six weeks. We'd been shown a dismal, temporary accommodation to stay in whilst our house underwent a renovation. Our inspection of this found walls running with damp, curtains covered in mildew and armies of millipedes negotiating the walls like some bizarre, interactive Laura Ashley wallpaper. On seeing the tears trickle down our children's faces, we'd dismissed the Plan B instantly and opted to work around the transitional renovation period instead in our own place.

Bit by bit, the house at Bomu Crescent got worse, as things often do prior to getting better. The tired kitchen, once functional, now resembled a strange non-descript space deplete of cupboards and worktops, without even a `fridge to indicate its former purpose. Only a dripping tap sprouting from an area under the window, gave any hints as to the function of this room.

❉

Weeks earlier on our first night in our new residence, we'd been startled looking out of the kitchen window into the darkness outside to be met with the smiling face of a friendly camp policeman flashing a mouthful of luminous teeth and brightest eyes out of the blackened night. I can still remember our hearts racing in fear, as my husband unlocked the padlock on the metal gate guarding the glass kitchen door and Wellington introduced himself. It turned out he'd taken it upon himself to place the security of our house and garden plants under his watchful eye, in the weeks prior to our arrival. He now produced a small notebook, detailing dates and times where he'd made inspections and some specifics of his findings and naturally was looking for some kind of monetary compensation for his trouble. He explained that he'd fended off intruders intent on removing any unfixed item from the property and that he had caught red-handed a pair of gardeners digging up prized plants from our garden. The evidence of his diligence was displayed in detailed accounts, neatly handwritten into his notebook rivalling any Scotland Yard investigation, and we conveyed our thanks by handing him a bundle of crumpled Niara notes. We'd been introduced to the Nigerian currency, the Niara, on arrival in Port Harcourt where we'd been met by an old friend from our previous Oman posting. Aware of the slow pace of the settling-in system in Nigeria, she'd decided to come to offer a friendly face and to lend us a bundle of cash to tide us over the first few days. I'll never forget the sight of that bundle, weighty, more than two hands high and laced up in old string. It required the use of a rucksack to contain it; forget any ideas of slipping a few notes into a handbag. As I thanked her profusely for her generosity in lending us such a large sum of money, she pointed out that the value of it was only about £60.

❉

In Bomu Crescent, our living room, a large airy room with deep windows overlooking a lush tropical garden and two sets of French doors, was soon reduced to a mere transiting hall, a room necessary to pass thorough only to get to our four-person bedroom facility. Floor tiles now ripped up left a tacky residue, which meant that every walk across the sticky surface caused a multitude of detritus to adhere to shoes; it was necessary to strip them clean from time to time, when the protrusions around the sides of the soles became too irritating, to focus on walking. This no-man's land also now housed our ῾fridge and unplumbed toilets waiting to be resettled in soon-to-be-newly-tiled bathrooms.

In the end, even the sanctuary of our bedroom retreat was broken with the smashing of the tiles in the en-suite as the sanitation refurbishment worked its way into every corner. There were days when it was quite possible to hold hands with someone in the garden whilst seated on the loo, if one were so inclined. I tried as best I could to banish thoughts of how many creepy crawlies would be thinking the same and tired to remain focused on a splendid result.

We had arrived in Nigeria to a camp at its social peak and occasional glimpses out of the security-grilled windows of our house would offer up clues to the revelling which we were not yet a part of. I remember clearly a certain shock at seeing one of my neighbours, a phoenix who had risen from the ashes in this crazy place, cycle past our house in a sparkling evening gown and pink feather boa floating in the air behind her. I watched her in awe and noticed the joy that she radiated with every spin of the wheels. Evidently, once the learning curve was negotiated, this place held some promise but not yet; I was not in the mood to party yet. Partying was the last thing on my mind. I was consumed still by the grief of recently losing my dear and lovely dad to what turned out to be an insurmountable battle with cancer and was deeply mourning his loss, as well as the loss of the sweet family I used to know, who'd spiralled off in opposing directions unable to come to terms with the event and the enormity of their grief.

Chapter 4
The Saddest Farewell

My dad had been a diminutive giant. A man of the most remarkable compassion and modesty, who most certainly had never stopped to contemplate the impact he made on those he touched or the devastation his passing would create. He was the only male of our house, our hero, and he coped admirably with being surrounded by us four women and our many female dramas. A passionate golfer, he had a particular talent for the game resulting in a low single-figure handicap, with a balance and consistency to his swing which mirrored his general steady way of being. In a house of three daughters, he didn't have any regular offers of caddy help; but we all admired the depths of his unwavering passion for, what I know now, to be the most special of sports. We used to fight to clean the mud and grass cuttings from his shoes and scrub his clubs, eager to please and to do our bit to demonstrate our approval and enormous respect for him. We'd watch him regularly in the kitchen, honing his swing and sinking putts with imaginary clubs, whilst the evening meal was in its final minutes of cooking.

He'd been an all round talent, sporty, intelligent, sharp as a pin and highly successful in business and yet with a self-deprecating way that sought out for praise the strengths of others he came into contact with instead of his own. Small in stature, he'd been signed up as a youth to play for one of the major Scottish football teams, but had succumbed to the fragility of his petite 5 feet 2 inch frame and a weakness in his ankles that could speed him deftly past the rest of the field, regularly capturing the ball, but which could not take the permanent pounding of lengthy training sessions. His budding football career had met with an untimely end.

Many years later, it was his entire body that had now catastrophically failed him, when his thirst for life and for living was still very much in evidence. He withered in front of us, his girls, his home team, until the light was no longer able to shine from his tired eyes and his body was unrecognisable, ravaged by the disease which was to claim him. He'd fought his greatest battle, with tubes and drains, fevers that had his body drenched and rigours that had him uncontrollably and violently shaking. In his final days he'd been watching newcomer Tiger Woods about to secure his first Masters' victory, but became too unwell to see him complete the final holes. He'd also missed the commentator, his favourite, announce from the screen with the greatest of ironic timing, "I'd like to send my best wishes to Alex, up there in hospital in Edinburgh. Get well soon, Alex."

I remember, next day, going in to see him and seeing the brightness wash over his face as he declared Tiger to be "phenomenal". It struck me how much that few minutes epitomised my lovely dad. As sick as anyone I'd ever seen, gaunt, jaundiced and hauntingly unwell and with teeth that now looked alarmingly over-sized for his face as he'd struggled to get the word "phenomenal" out. Even in this hopeless state, he was full of enthusiasm and admiration for this latest golfing prodigy and respect for someone performing above and beyond, just as he'd always done himself. To this day, each time I use or hear the word "phenomenal" I mentally punch the air to salute our absent and greatest hero.

Fifteen years have since passed, but tears come to my eyes like raindrops head-on in a storm that won't blink away, thinking of that wretched time and of having to let our soldier go like that. It seemed to me that there had been a mistake made and that someone who possessed such gentleness shouldn't have been placed in the grips of a cruel reaper like cancer. My dad's response, I know well, would have been "Why not me?", never wanting to see himself as special. Even the slippers we brought to his hospital bed were to be the old familiar leather ones, dainty and immaculately stitched, but which were understated, subdued and sitting quietly and modestly beneath the heavy ironwork of the hospital bed.

Dad was not unaccustomed to the odd hang-up, the sort of thing that those who strive for perfection are prey to. When we were summoned in for what turned out to be his last dramatic breaths, he was perturbed that the auxiliary had placed a lunch tray of now cold food on his table that he desperately wanted rid of. Who could blame him? It was like some macabre timing from a black comedy. But that was my dad, fighting to the bitter end to live and die according to his rules and his exacting standards.

The horrific unfolding of his death was something that we were ill-prepared for and by no means the peaceful slipping away that concludes so many tear-jerker films. As the end credits rolled, he seemed to be in pain, ironically fighting for air and for life-giving oxygen, supplied to him eventually via a face-mask by a kind nurse who recognised the stage of dying he was at. Later, as the nightmare scene replayed over and over in my mind, no matter how much I tried to change channels, I pondered that dying seemed strangely akin to the pain and drama of childbirth, although with only the one giving life and tears of joy. I still recall his last few words, the only thing that seemed to offer hope to the dismal situation: "All is well"; and then his blood stopped pulsing, and far too quickly our warm fatherly figure slipped from a body that now lay stone-cold and icy. I gave him one last hug and farewell, a chilled, lifeless hug where he was for once not able to wrap reassuring arms around me, or any of us, but could only lie still and motionless, his leather slippers neatly at his bedside and family photos and drawings made for him by his grandchildren carefully stuck to the outside of his locker.

Poignantly, my two sisters had regularly brought their expanding bodies in on each hospital visit, expectant with children who would never have the pleasure of learning from their dear Granddad, or of being able to light up his face with their smiles. It seemed that if you were to be writing the script, you wouldn't have written it with such an ending, coming prematurely when so much of the happy story was still to be told.

My mum and sisters were lost and devastated by his passing. The inconceivable had happened and we were no longer able to benefit from endless kindness and wisdom that had always been freely given, as well as the particularly special energy that he radiated. As often happens in times of trauma like this, our little family blew apart, splintered into wounded fractions and quickly became disjointed. Things had come to such a head that, soon after his passing, I no longer had contact with my twin sister and her family, living only twenty minutes away from our home in Edinburgh, and could not turn to her for her customary sisterly support. I was both haunted by reflections of the horrors around me in Nigeria and with the horrors I'd left behind. Escape was hard to find. Widowed and bereft my mum was unable to find any comfort from her sorrow, one sister struggling in the middle and my twin and her family now estranged from us.

Everywhere there were reminders of a cavernous gap in the family. I remember the little things, like finding his glasses in neat cases scattered round the house, the jackets still with his smell and the golf shoes, moulded from wear into the shape of his feet and stuck with grass and mud from happier days, even containing evidence of his last round. He'd often hold out a foot to us all and tell us girls how magnificent he thought his feet were, perfect and petite and a tiny man's size five which caused him and my mother no end of shopping challenges. Latterly, in hospital, he'd sit with his legs raised on a chair, feet protruding from a hospital blanket, grotesquely swollen and unrecognisable. I'd quietly ponder how he must have been feeling to see such graphic evidence of the toxins that now surged through his body, transforming his limbs, and I was consumed by the thought of the intense discomfort he was so stoically bearing.

❈

Now in this austere place, the Niger Delta, the traumas of my dad's death and this chaotic and emotional family back home kept me in the solitude of my own company. I didn't feel ready yet to embrace new life and make new friends and instead chose to dwell on those I'd lost, from close bonds left a flight away on our previous post, to sisters, to the good old family now faded and not least to the loss of my beloved dad. I couldn't introduce myself as Lynne who'd just lost so much that she held dear, and yet to say nothing seemed to offer no explanations of the ghost of I person I felt I'd become. I found it easier to keep social interaction at arm's length.

Creating one's nest in a company assigned house cannot be understated. Life takes on a different lustre when you have, as a minimum, your own personal belongings cozied into a home that has been allocated randomly to you. The house is selected, marked up on some white board with your name or company 'indicator code' beside it for the duration of a posting, and handed over to you now void, save residual history left by previous tenants from years gone by .

The notion that you can't really properly relax into life and settle until your container worldly goods is unpacked is one that seems always to go against my spiritual bent, which tells me that all that I require for my wholesome, complete living can be derived from within. I have the feeling that an energetic component is at play and the notion that a vivid blue sofa and under-loved cabinet from the company loan float do not send out the same positive vibes as our own familiar furnishings do. Perhaps it is as basic as that, the idea that your own chosen items have a certain empathy and harmony resonating from them, which just makes life feel lighter and more friendly.

It quickly seemed that it would be important in Nigeria to have a haven from the darkness that pervaded the outside, even during the sunlight hours. Each of the houses in the Nigerian camp had a 'Boys' Quarters' - or BQ as it is referred to - where traditionally any staff belonging to the household would live. This alone was a strange concept but we also learned that the BQ at the foot of our particular garden had a melancholy history that would need the heaviest application of feng shui to counteract. Rumour had it, and confirmed in a published book, that the shower room there had been used as a torture chamber during the Biafran War, a period of time when the entire camp had been taken over by military personnel. The war lasted from 1967-1970 and stemmed from political conflict created by the breaking away of the south-eastern provinces of Nigeria to form the Republic of Biafra. A million citizens had died during the two-and-a-half-year war as a result of fighting and famine, until the Federal Military Government declared a ceasefire and Biafra was once more merged into Nigeria.

The house began to shape up and seemed appreciative of the warm, sand tone now adorning the living-room walls and the peaceful pistachio of the bedrooms. We had a few trials along the way, in particular a plumber who was insistent that the loos should be raised on wooden gloss-painted platforms to facilitate the contortions of the local piping. It was at times difficult enough to get two little boys to wee with more accuracy and less splashing, and the idea that their aim would now be from the foot of a flight of steps, with the throne aloft and distant, filled me with horror.

We lived for six weeks on tuna sandwiches made on a chopping board in the bedroom and whilst my husband and the boys were able to leave the chaos of the house for periods of time, as project-overseer I was more or less confined to the sofa in the corner of the bedroom for the duration of the renovation work. One day, I'd specifically requested that the noxious glue, freshly smeared over the entire living-room floor and stretching its sticky expanse into the hallway and bathrooms, would be covered in new lino tiles on my return from school with the boys. I was only mildly reassured by the pledges from the workmen that the floor would be in an entirely completed state by the deadline. I later arrived back to a sticky mayhem and tiles lying in unopened boxes, and with two children desperately needing to access the toilet some yards down a glue-filled alley. The men eventually scrambled to attention and seeing my despair and sensing the gravity of the emergency, even the joinery and painting departments suspended all to assist, dealing out tiles like experienced croupiers in a casino. With some embarrassment, eventually the boys step-stoned their way to relief. At least we had a central pathway of tiles and I remained hopeful that one day this would be eventually joined up to the adjacent walls and would resemble a proper floor covering.

There were a few renovation issues that had slipped our attention, one of which was the inclining of our bath in the master en-suite to enable 'easier drainage', and the other being a hole that had accidentally been punctured in the bath, now newly installed and tiled-in, set off with fine mahogany skirting and bathroom furniture. I was the fortunate member of our family to be given the treat of commissioning the new splendid bathing facility. All was going swimmingly until the water level reached the crucial ten centimetres mark and began to spurt like blood from an artery. This being Nigeria, however, and this being after several weeks of uncomfortable and dusty living conditions, I continued to bathe with a toe wedged into the outlet, stemming the bleed long enough for me to relax in the warm water as well as continuing to stop my advance toward the plughole at the end of the sloping floor of the bath. This technique of remaining at the top of the bath and resisting the gravitational pull to the plughole would be perfected over years of continuous bathing in such a steeply inclined bath.

During my commissioning of the bathing facility, I'd marvelled at how any addition of soap to the tea-brown-stained water that came out of our taps had the added benefit of turning the water a bright and not unattractive turquoise blue. You had to get used to the tap-water in Nigeria, with its brownish-orange hue. We'd once had the misfortune to have two worms come cascading out before our horrified faces and slithering, shocked, past our loaded toothbrushes. We knew, however, that we were the lucky ones with water that came running from taps whatever colour it was, and that we didn't have to walk for miles to fetch such a basic necessity like so many there had to do. In Nigeria, even a first class degree scholar couldn't be guaranteed running water or regular power.

Our camp was the seat of luxury in comparison to the challenges for survival being dealt with on the outside. Our water was most often constant, although we'd had to get used to regular daily power outages. At first it was shocking to have the house plunged into blackness and to have to rely on candles and get used to the eerie silence that descends when clattering and elderly air conditioning units take time out. Often the termination of noise is the thing that alerts you most to its presence, particularly with such a regular and background noise as a cooling air conditioning unit. I've often thought the same about great art and how the measure of its ability to command a room with its energy is felt by its lack when it is removed.

Occasionally the power outages would test our patience, particularly if you'd been engrossed in some live satellite sporting event. I still recall a football match during one of the World Cup events and Scotland unusually finding themselves in the position of leading. With the opponents raising their game in defiance, the house at Bomu Crescent was plunged into blackness. Unfortunately, on this occasion, by the time our electrical items buzzed into life again some two hours later, Scotland had been thoroughly defeated with a miserable 3-1 result. I couldn't help feeling partly responsible for not having been able to offer a more reliable support for our nation.

As we ascended the learning curve, we realised there were ways to raise the priority of one's house in the queue for generator selection. Eventually, my husband would go to the generator that served our houses and inform the engineers there that numbers 2 and 5 were on home-leave and request that they be darkened in order for illuminations to temporarily be sent to us. As if to demonstrate the ability of people to adapt to changing circumstances, often power outages went by almost unnoticed. You'd be sitting at a dinner in someone's house, engaging in banter, with everyone seemingly oblivious to the darkening ambiance and the candle lighting becoming now more of a necessity than a luxurious, romantic touch. Conversations never missed a beat.

At home we'd opted to sleep with a fan above our bed instead of having our sleep disturbed by the sound of a particularly noisy air conditioner sited under the window in the bedroom. At times, however, with the fluctuations in our power voltage, it was debatable which was the lesser of the evils. Many a night, semi- awake, I'd lie there with the sound of propellers slowing down to trickle and then whizzing to top speed and wish the helicopter would land, wherever it was. Very often the power would be so crazily varied that electric light bulbs would glow from intense halogen white to a dim gas light effect. These 'brown-outs' would wreak havoc on electrical equipment, and items without surge protectors would meet an early demise.

When I reflect on Nigeria, one of the other things along with the padlocks that comes to mind is the sight of the local people carrying everything on their heads, always perfectly balanced as they walk proudly erect. Water was most commonly carried in this way in big plastic containers, or bundles of firewood or baskets laden with vegetables. I think we Oyibos quietly marvelled at this local skill, knowing that loads would never reach intended destinations intact if we were to be the bearers, or certainly not in this elegant manner. On one occasion, I saw a gentleman walk with his bowler hat upside down on top of his head, unconventionally inverted, signifying that the he was 'carrying' the hat as opposed to 'wearing' it.

Eventually, our house started to fill up with furnishings we'd had made locally, sometimes with greater success than others. There was the dining table, large, round and according to my design should have had a 'slightly uneven' hand-finished surface and, very importantly, be left unvarnished. After several weeks in the workshop, the day of delivery came and the table was struggled into our house, brown and glossy and with a surface akin to the craters on the moon. It was like a slice of gigantic chocolate-dipped golf ball and completely unable to comply with its task of supporting items on its surface. Wine glasses were a disaster, while peas ran in circles and sauce dribbled off dinner plate edges. The only thing that our new table could safely handle was a generous, empty tea tray. Admittedly, my artistic design had been on the ambitious side for the unfortunate craftsmen to translate. I wasn't even entirely sure I understood my own brief, only that I knew I wanted our table to be a bit different and on that remit, it had matched my specifications to perfection; I've certainly never seen one like it before or since.

We also had a small mix-up with a couple of sofas that we'd had made, in a cool cream pre-dog owner's linen. The design echoed the boxy modern look we were after, but the size in inches from our drawings in centimetres made me feel even tinier than my 5 feet 2 inch frame and looked like props from a film set. We did have some glorious success with a coffee table and Rennie Mackintosh-inspired chairs made by a Nigerian gentleman married to a Glaswegian lady. It turned out he had actually seen the original chairs in the Mackintosh museum in Scotland. The chairs, solid hardwood, are still going strong and still accompany us on our travels. The coffee table unfortunately emitted an enormous bang one evening, mimicking a gunshot, a sound that we were becoming all too familiar with, and split from end to end.

It wasn't uncommon to find evidence of gunshots, in the form of spent shells that had fallen into the camp gardens and golf course areas. One or two bullets had made their way inside the residential houses, easily penetrating the tin roofs, and I know of at least one employee who arrived for work in the company's headquarters one day to find a bullet sitting on his 'To do' pile of the day's paperwork.

Chapter 5

Life in Port Harcourt, Nigeria

By now, life in Port Harcourt had begun to settle and the arrival of our sea freight and familiar furnishings helped to make the house at Bomu Crescent more ours and more of the essential safe haven that our family needed. We eventually surrendered our fight against the challenges we were facing on a daily basis and had started to relax into African ways. Surrender was the only way to preserve sanity here. Living for too long at loggerheads with the place brought your reserves down and some acceptance of such a change to life needed to be embraced. We began to shake outstretched hands of friendship that seemed more willingly given and to open our doors in reciprocation. Our new staff contingent were working in harmony with us and assisted in making life easier, if not at times positively luxurious, for the family. Charles, our driver, had an unwavering smile as wide as the grille of the car. He was a joy, always upbeat and cheery and smartly turned out for his chauffeuring job. Some days he would turn out in western attire, but I especially liked it when he proudly wore his local exotic outfits. One in particular, my favourite, flamboyantly made in intricate broderie anglaise and whiter than white, suited his charismatic personality well. Considering the less than fantastic laundry facilities available to him in the BQ, it was amazing that the fabric never lost its brilliance or its washing powder advertisement whiteness.

I remember one occasion when my sensitivities to his occasional decision to use our car for the transportation of his personal goods were overly attuned. Our car had begun to take on an unpleasant smell and it had become necessary on journeys to open the windows to allow some fresh air in to breathe. I'd asked Charles repeatedly if he'd been transporting dried fish, a local delicacy, which exuded a noxious odour not dissimilar to the interior of our car. He vehemently denied any such impropriety and some days later, disturbed by a metallic clattering noise outside, I looked out of the bedroom window to be met with the sight of Charles heaving the one remaining car seat out of our car. To my shamed face, he explained that he'd located a dead lizard wedged under a seat and this discovery had eliminated the source of the car stench. I congratulated him on his fastidiousness and went back inside the house horrified by the thoughts rising in my head that he may have placed the dead reptile in the car to cover his tracks. Nigeria did this to you. The notion that someone was trying to abuse your generosity kept personal safety and acceptability guards on high alert. Charles was well known and a well-loved member of the camp, having driven 'masters' safely for many years and I seem to recall that the lizard incident was the last problem we ever paid attention to.

Employment associations with oil companies did not make you exempt from the often infuriating petrol crisis in the country and, at times of fuel scarcity, Charles could be relied on to do his level best to get the car tank filled, even partially. Many a time things were so bad that he would sleep overnight in the car to maintain his place in the snaking queues. Even such extreme diligence on his part was often only able to secure us a mere trickle of fuel rationed out or enough to fill a small jerry can. As well as the obvious discomforts encountered sleeping in a petrol queue, things at times became volatile and dangerous as frustrations grew and the army would be deployed to police the situation.

Our staff contingent all dried their clothes outside, spread over bushes or hung up on rudimentary washing lines, Charles's ornate outfits included. For some reason, we Oyibos had to be most careful with the drying of laundry outside and our exterior washing line only ever served a decorative purpose. An especially extreme fly in this area of West Africa, the Tumbu bug, made the drying outdoors of clothes a perilous activity. These bugs lay their eggs in damp washing, soon hatching to larvae that could remain alive for two weeks. During that time, if the clothing came into contact with the skin these larvae burrowed into it. If you were unfortunate to be playing host to such an unwelcome visitor, the simplest home-cure solution was to apply some Vaseline to the reddened swelling and to cut off the supply of vital oxygen to the growing bug. The theory was that the maggot, positioned head first and rear out, would begin to reverse in search of air and would protrude far enough to be grabbed with some tweezers and pulled out. Unless items dried outside were thoroughly ironed to kill the eggs, or furiously tumble-dried, such a method of exterior drying was ill-advised. Several fellow ex-pats had been unfortunate to pick up these bugs from damp beach towels and ended up with loud angry sores, horrifically containing live maggots. I was fastidious in making sure all items of washing were tumbled and ironed to within an inch of their lives to avoid such nightmares. In certain cases, the dead creatures would need to be surgically removed from their human nest and the prospect of this ensured I applied the highest safety measures to the laundry tasks.

Blessing, our 'nanny' or house help, made sure hidden corners were regularly stirred and could be relied on to send any insect residents scurrying for cover and a rethink of their chosen abode. She was a bright, smiling character, with enough experience in domestic work, thankfully, to need little instructing. There were plenty of domestic staff incidents that did the amusement rounds across dinner tables. One friend had returned home one day to find a telephone number etched on the surface of her wooden bookcase and ruining the carefully waxed pine finish. The explanation went along the lines that the nanny hadn't wanted to spoil a fresh sheet of A4 paper, laid on top of the bookcase for this specific purpose, and had elected instead to write out 'phone details etched by biro into the soft pine, shipped by the owners from Aberdeen. Another tale, told frequently to an always shocked but eager audience, relayed details of one madam emptying her dishwasher to find her toaster and electric kettle inside, steaming hot and gleaming amongst the cleaned dishes.

Blessing's greatest crime was her full pitch gospel singing, delivered with the maximum capacity of her able lungs and which I ruthlessly cut down to a veritable hum. I'd felt callously cruel, like removing the song from the nightingale, but I have a sensitivity to noise and a concentration that fails to stay tuned amidst too much exterior distraction, particularly gospel singing. Whilst I appreciated the indication this gave that she was happy at her work, a peaceful environment and controlled sound are necessities for my functioning. Blessing also had an irritating tendency to wear any clothes I'd given her, regardless of the disparaging sizes or the suitability of a sequined top in which to perform dusting tasks. No matter how much strain was bearing against tight seams, or how sparkly the adornments, my attempts at middle-age Rock Star Chic would be paraded in front of my eyes and I'd wince at the reminders of a deviation in my customary sober dressing that I was trying my best to forget.

The garden, too, in the nurturing hands of Freedom and his two young boy assistants, was blossoming. From the last blade of grass and with sweeping machete chops, he'd carried out our directions for the landscaping and occasional radical turf and plant uproot, that told everyone but especially ourselves that we'd accepted our tenancy of the house at number 4 and were intent on making our mark. There's nothing like cultivating a new hedge to make you feel you have established yourself and set down roots in your new foreign abode. When I become overwhelmed by the desire to plant a little hedge, I always acknowledge it as a good sign.

The camp was an oasis of calm amidst a bursting and threatening city and I chose to expose myself to limited time in the outside world and its gut-wrenching sights. Traffic was often at a standstill and a shopping trip, which should have taken twenty minutes, could easily take three hours, giving plenty of opportunity for business to thrive in the long crawling queues of cars. According to safety precautions, 'sirs and madams' were transported in their locked vehicles by their trusted drivers. The awkwardness of having your fortunate life displayed like this to the much less fortunate, outside the toughened glass and seat-belted security, was as uncomfortable as walking past a homeless person in your own home town, with his small cardboard appeal for donations in his hand and shopping bags of decadence cutting painfully into your own.

Here in Nigeria the scale was much worse; beggars, limbless and motorised by paddling their flip-flopped hands along with their disfigured bodies balanced on skateboards, would often use slow-moving car door handles to aid their advance. Only the most shut-down and hardened heart would not be disturbed by witnessing the sight of their hands tapping the windows of your vehicle, in the desperate hope of some 'dash' or money being donated to them. As well as the skateboard men, there were the blind and disfigured bodies pushed along in wheelbarrows, barely able to hold out a sinewy hand for the life-giving money they were after. There were the mothers, with babies swaddled in rags and clutched tight to their chests, looking for anything that might be given out to make at least a small difference to their next 24 hours, if not to change their lives completely.

Plenty of able-bodied salesmen sauntered around, also vying for a place in this movable market, selling anything from driving licences to kebabs of barbequed Witchetty grubs. These grubs were large wood-eating moth larvae, resembling white caterpillars, which used to be gathered from decaying tree trunks and eaten. I was never tempted or brave enough to try them, but on each car trip made into town you would pass traders selling them toasted and browned, stacked up on kebab skewers being sold through car windows. I made a little promise to myself, which sadly I never did honour, to drive down the street on our last day throwing Niara out of the car into hands that would be bestowed good fortune for a few precious minutes. To give cash freely like this would have been a gesture suitable only for the last day in the country and would avoid expectations being held that, every time the 4 Bomu madame drove past, it would be a good thing to adhere limpet-like to her car. In the end it had seemed that this gesture fell sadly short of making any significant difference and might even cause scuffles as people fought to gather it, and I'd thought the better of the idea.

After a while you tried to de-tune to an extent from the harrowing sights of these unfortunate people in order to keep sane. It hit the core of your stomach to think that all the money you could throw out of the window and all the hugs your body was capable of surrendering would never be able to whisk these people away from their daily grind. I pledged to try my utmost to give my charitable donations, or to show kindness to as many people as I could, in one-to-one situations rather than to this frenzied needy mass, like tending a few plants in a greenhouse instead of a full-blown forest.

I recall one occasion mid-way thorough our posting where Charles, the driver, and I were in a familiar go-slow and to my right I spotted a small monkey chained to the belly of an ornately painted African truck, with brightly coloured gypsy livery carefully picked out in the metal panels. As we progressed at a miserable snail's pace, the monkey and I locked eyes through the car window and I saw the desperation in its face and a look that told me it recognised me as its saviour. I was moved to tears behind my sunglasses and horrified to find myself so caught up in the woes of a little monkey, when for as far as my eyes could see there was desperation etched on people's faces. Even the sight of the hammock slung underneath the truck, perilously close to the wheels and only just clearing the ground, in which a man was sleeping, didn't de-tune me from the plight of this little chained creature. The man had the free will, after all, and could walk away; the monkey was now some-one else's property and as such could only just barely turn in its chains to ease its sores. Freedom for the monkey was long gone.

We treated our staff kindly and with the respect that one deserves for carrying out a good and often excellent job, sometimes paying for roofs to be put on their village houses. At least we hoped this way our cash was going to go directly to a worthy cause. I'd once bought a new pair of shoes for a little girl who did odd gardening jobs around the camp and whose shoes were so worn down that the heel part was non-existent, her bare foot making contact with the ground on each step. Her mother thanked me for them as well as for some clothes and a few games that I'd given to her daughter. I'd felt good about being able to offer some modest help. However, the very next day, I saw the same girl wearing her old ripped shoes and breathed a defeated sigh of frustration. I'm not sure if my gifts had been sold to provide cash, but it made me sad to think that, whatever the reason, the root of the problem was a poverty so severe that survival action like that had to be taken. I don't think for one minute her mother wouldn't have been happier to see her child more practically shod, but other priorities took precedence.

That was one aspect of Nigeria that deflated and depressed many of us residents, comfortable in our kitted-out homes with little Britain, little USA and little Holland having been transported at great expense in stuffed shipping containers. I remember vividly one day mid-renovation, buying croissants from the 'bread lady', who came to the camp twice a week in the battered vehicle that doubled as her shop. That day I'd had more than a dozen workers busy in the house and I wanted to offer some little thanks to them, in a way that felt less vulgar than actual cash. Pleased to see the men happy with their chocolate croissants, I went outside again, just in time to catch the plumber deep in conversation with her. It turned out that although he was happy with the croissant he was animatedly negotiating a trade-in and upgrade for a more costly meat pie.

My goodwill sentiments instantly crumbled. If you were to give a finger, then an arm was required.

'Dashes' were a common practice in the country, an obligatory tip, and most times I wandered around with a few Niara in the rear pocket of my jeans for such tipping occasions. It was the expected custom and the tip always fell into open palms and was received most graciously. From time to time you would be stopped at road blocks, particularly in areas where the road was in such a poor state that potholes were large and difficult to negotiate and required dead-slow speed and skill of your driver. In such an area, it would be common to find yourself paying a 'dash' in response to a police stop, or exchanging money for a "What have you got for me?" I still smile recalling one time I'd forgotten my Niara, but had an old Hello magazine in the car. I used this as payment instead, leaving two policemen standing in the middle of the road, guns at jaunty angles on their shoulders, devouring the contents of the magazine and thrilled to have something in their hands that wasn't belonging to Nigeria but instead was imported. No disrespect to the quality of the Hello magazine's photo shots, but its content bore no real significance.

Currency in the country was about as far removed from the convenience of a debit card swipe as you could get. Soon after arrival, my husband was given a cash advance to enable us to buy some necessary white goods and had to go to the bank to collect the money. The denominations were so low, that to carry the pungent bundles of notes home required two suitcases. The smell of the money in Nigeria is something that is easily recalled along with the systems that had to be learned easily to count the bundles of notes required when purchasing a few bags of groceries. I devised a method of preparing bundles of amounts, folded with another note, as one would group with a rubber band. I'd sit with a glass of water to dip my fingers in as I rattled through bundle after bundle of notes, only stopping to lubricate the count with the water from the glass when my fingers became too dry to slide one grubby note past the next. The glass was a safety measure, as I'd been cautioned that 90% of the germs in the country could be found clinging to marinated notes and as such it was unwise to lick one's fingers whilst counting. The smell and colour of the notes was probably warning enough, in the same way that flamboyant red caterpillars that descended on certain trees in the camp every October with their yellow spots and large black, curving spikes sent out 'handle with care' signs. Note-counting is a skill I've still retained and one I still use on the very rare occasion nowadays that I've got more than a dozen pieces of monetary paper to count. Such a counting method is always met with curious looks by shop assistants, wondering if the skill has a drug-related or gambling history, and I wait until the bemused thought has sat in their heads, ready to burst, before offering up my Nigerian explanation.

The insect side of Nigeria was something to adjust to after years of relative safety in the Middle East, apart from a huge scorpion I very nearly put my hand on whilst checking to see if one of my plants was thirsty. My angels were with me that day, I'm certain of it. As I'd plunged my thumb in to test the soil for water content, I spied an open vent beside the window and instantly decided to inspect the plant. Without moving my thumb even a millimetre, I'd lifted the pot with my other hand close to eye level. My senses had been correct, nestled barely an inch from my thumb was a large shiny, black scorpion. It was over twelve centimetres long and with a menacingly primed tail arched over its armoured body. Despite knowing that it's the tiny, pale scorpions you have to fear most, I was terrified. I could sense a certain James Bond cinema tension envelope me. After some panicked `phone calls trying to discover what was the protocol in such situations, a kindly neighbour arrived with one year's experience and a bravery ahead of mine. I noticed when she arrived that she was rubber-gloved and brandishing a wooden spatula and I watched her quickly manage to coax the intruder into an empty coffee jar. It lived without food or air for weeks in this jar, ahead of me taking it still kicking to the clinic to donate as a specimen. People were occasionally stung by scorpions in Oman and it was sensible to adopt specific precautions such as the shaking of trainers before putting one's foot inside. An unfortunate lady was unlucky enough to have been stung twice by a scorpion that had hidden itself in the pocket of a blouse hanging in her wardrobe and which she'd unwittingly put on. Mindful of this tale, I'd added a pocket-shaking ceremony to my daily dressing list followed by shakes of my footwear to empty out any possible wildlife.

In Nigeria, we'd been fortunate to have had minimal encounters with the insect life on the camp and managed to cope with the infuriating but not sinister little millipedes that were always intent on entering the house. There was often evidence of dead little curled up sections and an indication that, no matter how you tried to exclude them, there would always be an entry point into your house. It was recommended that the 'camp services' people came and put purple crystals around the house from time to time to halt the invasion. I always have a sense that it's better somehow to co-exist in nature with beasties such as these, feeling that measures involving pesticides and the like are a bit like trying to deal with the problem by bashing the invaders with a mallet. It might prove an excellent targeted quick kill for a few, but has the disadvantage of sending the rest of the pack scurrying deeper into the confines of your house and exacerbating the problem.

We'd had a mirror in the bathroom, framed in the abundant mahogany of Nigeria but with a plywood backing which crackled mysteriously every time you tried to relax in the bath. Later inspection revealed a bug tunnelling itself a complex warren out of the softwood back. As one would expect in a camp that was a leafy enclosure compared to a muddy city outside, many snakes also sought to reside uninvited alongside us. There were great tales of people finding them in frying pans in cupboards and of them falling out of air conditioner grilles, to keep you terrified. We were fortunate only to witness one or two in the garden. One themed evening as my husband and I were headed out in our car dressed in mediaeval gear, we'd had to brake hard to allow a fat snake with a body thicker than a generous thigh to complete its journey over the road. There was also occasional evidence of slithery trails through the bunkers on the golf course that kept you on your toes and had you executing your escape from the sand as briefly as possible utilising the sand wedge with surprising skill. Over the years we'd caught sight of several deceased serpents on the tarmac road around our camp, normally having met with painful ends. One of our sons kept a pictorial demise record of them all in his sketch book, tracking whether they'd been squashed or decapitated, and shaded in coloured pencil so as to leave no room for doubt. I remember inviting one new arrival, fresh from London, for coffee and her mentioning between homemade shortbread biscuits that on leaving her house she'd spotted a huge luminous green snake hissing and rearing at her and was this normal? I'd replied that this was certainly not a normal sighting and had been happy to be able to answer with such certainty, basking in my ex-newcomer status and most relieved that she lived far away from my house. Lesley was on her first overseas posting and, trying to adjust to a life as an at-home mum, had thrown herself into the amateur dramatic side of the camp life. In her early few weeks she'd already made an impact on the acting fraternity, making the certainty of the pantomime Cinderella casting, to a rival, look less sewn up then we'd all thought.

Knowledge of creature life like that always kept me on my guard and I always paid the greatest respect to warnings, such as the pesky fire ants returning for their season bent on burning unsuspecting victims with their acid kiss. During their season, I had developed an almost paranoid fear of going out at night lest I became one of their victims. You never felt their presence at the time, only much later when an angry rash begun to manifest was your failure to avoid their strike revealed.

Whatever could be said of Nigeria, life was never dull or boring and we had plenty to contend with to keep us living on somewhat of an edge. We lived with constant security issues residing in the back of our heads, lodged so deeply that only years later post-Nigeria did you observe yourself forgetting to consider what might be happening behind your back. Occasionally, there would be trouble flared and we camp residents and workers, trying to make the short drive off-camp to the office, would be confined to barracks. The wonderful plus point of such imposed incarceration was that I'd have an eager supply of willing hands to whom to delegate the latest scenery painting tasks and to ensure the pressure of completion deadline was removed, smugly, way ahead of curtain-up.

As well as the occasional violence and just as disturbing, was the noise pollution that we suffered 24 hours of the day. We'd regularly hear screeching sirens of police cars as they pushed their way through the tail-to-tail traffic. Their cars emitted a blood-curdling scream, which took years for my ears to de-tune from after leaving. To me it portrayed a violence so unnecessary that it came to symbolise much of what was not right about this city and entire country. The police trucks, open at the back, would have several policemen perched on the edge, each armed and brandishing wooden batons in the air. They would spare no mercy as they smashed and bullied their way past traffic-jammed cars, smashing windscreens on their way. Helpless motorists could only sit and accept the punishment meted out, knowing that by a fate of time and location coinciding today was their day for this vehicle damage to be inflicted. Their only crime was to occupy a section of road at a particular moment and they would have to repair, with ungainly stitches like post-operational sutures, the broken screens, a style sported by so many others on the highways. To me, it seemed the peacekeeping police force could have done a much better job of uniting the place and countrymen, but chose instead to wield a violence that was akin to an animal attacking its own tail, senseless, self-destructive and needlessly cruel.

I had a great deal of admiration for almost all of the Nigerians I came across or observed at a distance, handling humiliation without grudge and holding heads high and proud even if in the unfortunate position of being bare shod and without a decent roof over their heads. This spirit I admired and was one that should have been able to take a richly fertile and oil–wealthy great nation unwaveringly forward, but instead seemed to have brought little gain. I'd reflect on how my fellow Scots would respond to having the windows of their prized cars defaced in such a way and thought of the riots that would ensue, a far cry from this quiet acceptance of the way things were here.

My husband called home one day from his work in the jungle. Despite a terrible signal and badly crackled line, I could sense the shock in his voice and visualised the paleness that must now have surely descended over his face to accompany such an angst-ridden pitch. As well as the kind-hearted there are, as in any society, fractions and groups fighting their causes, often targeting wealthy industry. They vent their general hatred and are often no longer sure of the actual cause they stand for, only a grim need for violence. This day, it was my husband's time to be in the wrong place. During our first year in the country, his work had involved him going each day by helicopter deep into the jungle and to a gas plant that he was overseeing the construction of. By any accounts, his years of engineering studies at university must have offered up few clues as to the promise of such exciting working locations. For months he'd taken the helicopter to work as one might take the bus or underground and the idea, once strange and risky, had now become normal for him. Occasionally he'd come home with amusing tales for the family, such as the time a Royal Python was found dead on his work site and he'd explained that a ritual must take place now to appease the gods and to bestow good fortune on the gas plant. There were to be donations of cases of beer, London Gin and at the foot of a long list of beverages and godly requests the payment of a large sum of money. Appeasing gods was never a cheap affair.

On this day there had been tension in the air on his arrival at site, which had begun to escalate and after lunch had eventually turned into a full-blown riot. Apparently, there were hundreds of locals, brandishing machetes and chanting their tribal voices to a level that reached fever-pitch. My husband, the only westerner on the site, was bundled into an office portacabin by thoughtful local colleagues, aware that his presence would further inflame an already violent situation. The police arrived and guns were fired, killing two of the rioters, until eventually the violence dissipated and the crowds dispersed, satisfied to have been noticed albeit nothing achieved.

Some time later, my husband and his colleagues were flown by helicopter back to the clinic on the company base, situated near the camp and treated for shock. My husband arrived home much later visibly shaken and took some time to recover from his ordeal, wearing his pale mask for several post-traumatic days. The overwhelming threat of such a number of voices shouting in unison and with a repetitive African beat had been terrifying for him and probably the only time in the duration of our Nigerian posting that any of us felt in real and life-threatening danger.

Chapter 6

Elephant Encounter in Gabon

In Gabon, I'd answered the old beige `phone on the varnished window-sill beside the makeshift pen holder. It was Helen. "Just to let you know, there's an elephant in our back garden right now. I thought you might be interested!" My husband happened to be home at the time and we'd instantly jumped into the car and headed off on the two minute drive, knowing that at this time of the evening and with darkness falling, as the African blanket that descended nightly and always suddenly from the sky, it would be too dangerous to go on foot.

Sure enough, there was no mistaking, adjacent to Helen's house and intent on wrapping its trunk around an inadequate shrub to strip leaves, which in one sweeping movement were folded and parcelled into its mouth, was our first elephant, a powering giant more brown than grey and with its back reaching to the eaves of the house. It didn't seem feasible that these vegetarian nibbles would be enough to sustain such a hulk of an animal and we marvelled at the volumes that must be consumed daily to keep the beast alive. In the safety of the car, we both observed and exchanged appreciative thoughts that Helen had remembered us newcomers, especially as this was in the heat of evening meal preparation time. She was visible inside the house, cautiously stealing glimpses of the animal, flitting between hot hob and window, regardless of the fact that after thee years of life on the camp she was accustomed to such sightings. As it occupied itself with this raw, leafy buffet, plodding from bush to bush and making almost silent progress, it barely stopped to notice us in our highly un-camouflaged, white 4 x 4, loudly declaring our recent arrival status, with its aroma of new rubber.

We'd heard so much about these camp inhabitants and had pondered when and where we might encounter our first specimen. We'd adopted the company safety policy for such meetings of man, metal and beast and switched off our car headlights, leaving the engine running for escape purposes, and watched from a safe distance. It was easy to be lulled into a false sense of security, assuming that these animals were tamed and just as harmless as the cute wooden carvings, with their roughly hewn trunks and implanted little white tusks, that trotted along many a resident's bookcase here, or the furry imitations snuggled in bed along with the camp's children. It was important to resist the inclination to encroach beyond reasonable safety distances and not to step into the danger zone, especially in a brand new shiny car, with part-payment to be completed.

There appears to be no family here in Gabon without their own personal tales of brushes with danger with these wandering camp giants. People have had tusks smash through house windows, or mosquito-netted patios, sending the residents fleeing for safety. Many have had to run for their lives chased by elephants, furious that the 'Welcome' door mats don't apply to them. Occasionally, cars and drivers are targeted for toying with and occupants of cars can only sit motionless, engines on and lights off until the danger has become bored and wandered off, like a menacing character from a Steven Spielberg thriller. Evidence of these encounters is visible in the form of dents, bashes and crazed glass on many of the 4 x 4 cars driven around here and always serves as a safety reminder.

We have a lone, mad elephant stalking the camp these days and causing mayhem and a destructive trail in his wake. Not content with rifling through our litterbins, perched on their metal poles and encased, he has turned his attention to causing cyclonic damage, uprooting fences and trees in his path. As one of the dog-walking fraternity, night-time pre-bed wees are becoming tinged with peril and, added to by worries of cobras possibly lurking under evening bushes and of millions of malaria-ridden mosquitoes gathering in the pool of light from the outside bulb, my personal elephant-alert status is at the brightest red. One of our neighbours was chased when out on such a mission recently and, as the story goes, had to run three times around his vehicle before he could escape to safety. The dog is seemingly still visibly shaken and the dents to the car contain forensic clues as to the authenticity of the incident.

A few nights earlier we'd attended a small safety briefing on the camp, open to all but of highest importance to newcomers who needed to be made aware of certain 'things' here in the jungle. We were fortunate enough to have one of the world's leading wildlife experts living on our camp and working for the Gabon branch of the world-renowned Smithsonian Institute. With several years of intense study in the bio-diverse area, his advice was the reference point we all looked to. There was unwavering respect for a man who has spent so much of his life enduring uncomfortable weeks and nights on location and taking venomous risks to glean information to help us all. In addition, despite his French nationality, he was a natural English language comic, always sensing the exact timing to inject his humour into the proceedings, in the way his specimens might add the element of surprise into their attack.

The briefing began with an overhead slide show, illustrating the company safety policies and security and evacuation measures put in place, should the unlikely occur and we had to pack our 15 kilos of favoured items and flee. Unlike Nigeria, when such evacuation briefings were taken in verbatim by a concerned audience, with notes made and questions asked, the briefing in Gabon was only half listened to. A storm was passing overhead and the sound of the rain on the metal roof of the presentation hall, coupled with the perfect lines of rainwater gathering in its corrugated gutters and pouring in metallic-looking rivulets like some expensive water feature into the small swimming pool outside, was too distractingly beautiful to revert eyes to a slide show of company logos and acronyms.

Interest was only mildly restored when images of French paratroopers who'd made parachute landings into the school sports field, rehearsing evacuation procedures, began to fill the screen. Somehow, seeing men on video dropping out of the sky like that and into an area regularly passed and familiar to us all, brought home the frightening reality and bravery of heaving oneself out of an open 'plane, with only a fabric sail and a few ropes to guide you down to your safety.

I reflect that such regular safety mock-ups must be incredibly exciting happenings for a sleepy hollow like our little camp here and must provide dinner and bar conversation for weeks. On a normal basis, we are used only to the sounds of the two little `planes that make the regular trips between the capital Libreville, Port Gentil, the terminal base of Rabi set in deep jungle and our own residential Yenzi Camp and work areas. Regardless of where your house is located, the small `planes fly low over your roof, close enough to display clear numbers and letters painted on the bodywork of the fuselage, if not the detailed expression on the pilot's face. On occasions, when a take off coincides with me being momentarily occupied domestically at the kitchen sink, I find myself declaring out loud to a dog who doesn't comprehend but who wags his tail in any case, that there goes Marijka, Paola and the like and my hopes for them to have a good holiday and welcome break from our remoteness here. I send out my wishes for them to enjoy the restaurants, cappuccinos, malls and importantly fruit and vegetable abundance of supermarket aisles, like people who have arrived from outer space and never seen such goodies before.

Eventually, with the closure of that section of our briefing and the arrival of a heavy cool box, things started to look up and our interest was quickly regained. Our expert began to educate us as to the profusion, type and danger of the snakes, living alongside us in the area. I knew snakes were most common occurrences in Gabon and also was prepared to be alarmed by the briefing, but was taken aback to find a striking cobra glaring out of the first colourful slide. There was to be no softly-softly approach, starting with the non-dangerous and increasing in venom with each new slide. This ghoulish image, along with the various text details surrounding the picture, spelt out its extreme danger status and made me shiver. Cobras are the most feared species in Gabon and also one of the most common, so I considered it incredibly out of character and brave of me to be, minutes later, handling a real, albeit dead and frozen specimen, passed round the room. The thing was thick, black and coiled up, and the sight of its pinched mean face and yellow tipped head, made all the hairs on my neck stand to attention. I attempted to offload the now defrosting serpent to the gentleman on my left, but he, along with the two beside him, refused to have a more intimate encounter with the deadly beast than observation at several feet offered. And so, with panic rising in my chest and my calmness timing out, my husband plucked the thing from my grasp and sent it on its way along the front row of keen handlers.

It was explained to us that nobody could die of a cobra bite, here in the Yenzi camp environs, so long as you were within 2 - 3 hours of the clinic and life-giving anti-venom. A cobra kills by causing paralysis and eventually it is the inability to breathe and asphyxia that causes death. This I found to be only mildly reassuring, counter-balanced by the information that cobras, unlike most other snakes, are not fearful of people and in fact will elect to invade the territory of people.

Next out of the cool box and simultaneously displayed on the screen was a viper, more timid and shy than the cobra and with venom that once injected could take 2 - 3 days to kill you by melting your flesh. Time enough to write parting emails to loved ones and to brush up one's affairs, or perhaps even to get a clinic visit scheduled and a dose of anti-venom administered. One by one, frozen and increasingly less frozen specimens were removed from the cool box and shown round the room. My initial bravery receded now as the rigid, iced bodies had warmed up into strange floppy life and I, along with the timid gentlemen to the left, passed up the opportunity for a closer introduction. A stunning green snake, alive and tweezer-ed between skilled thumb and fingers beamed out of the screen. "Very, very rare," our expert told us, and with no anti-venom on the market for its deadly bite, it had been found two days previously on the terminal beside the offices. A bite from this rare beast, he informed us, would cause death by haemorrhage. With his mastery of English and of snakes, our expert continued to tease us with such stories and to reinforce the point that sooner or later we'd be making our very own live, unfrozen encounters with very common or very, very rare specimens, venomous or not. The horned viper, with its fat belly and strikingly beautiful markings, that I couldn't help thinking would look fabulous belted over a sombre black outfit, casual but chic, is a particularly nasty beast. This creature lies in wait and can easily be trodden on, leading most often to a bite and a trip to the clinic for an antidote to its poison.

The last snake slides were of pythons, not dissimilar in markings to a handbag I owned, with its worn khaki leather body and a glistening python fastening snaking down over the zip, offset with unusual fabric lacing and silver loop details. For the moment I've switched allegiance to my jungle handbag, with the folded leather pockets, for practical and safety measures. The last thing I want to do is to enrage and provoke for revenge any brother or sisters of my snake-embellished bag lurking nearby. We sat silent to tales of python encounters on the camp and I winced along with my husband at the knowledge that Travis would now be on the radar of any python in the vicinity, with their ability to smell a cat or dog from kilometres away. Several cats have met with untimely ends in this manner and our expert's assistant gave a detailed account of a camp python that had recently vomited a cat.

One local Gabonese man, who grew and sold limited vegetables for our consumption, their roots snuggled in elephant dung fertilizer at best and human fertilizer possibly, had lost his dog the previous year to a python. The story goes that he had to call for assistance as the python had invaded his plantation in the night and swallowed his dog whole. The poor beast had been on guard dog duty and had been chained up to a metal elephant-protection fence. All that was visible as dawn broke was the python, with its distended belly struggling against the chain which was still secured around the dog's neck, now inside its belly and simultaneously tethered to its metal post. One can only imagine the horror of the poor man who tied his dog up in the evening, to find it morphed into a two metre python by daybreak.

Our man proceeded to tell us similar tales of chained dogs meeting their demise in the jaws of Nile crocodiles, also common in the area. I have a friend here whose dog spent its last few blissful minutes of life swimming in shallow sea water at one of the beaches, whilst its careful owners set up a barbeque, unaware their pooch had been taken as croc-snack. Our wildlife man cautioned that so much focus is paid to the snake and elephant dangers here, that the risks posed by such Nile crocodiles are often over-looked. There is a small annexe to our camp, located a few kilometres away, fitted in as we are around a small lake. Unlike our own, their lake is known to contain several of these Nile crocodiles and concerns had grown so high for the risks posed to innocent and unsuspecting people sitting beside the calming waters, with an evening beer in their hands, that a little 'Attention: Crocodiles' sign had been erected. A four-metre croc has the appetite to eat a whole person and it is believed the giants there are over seven and as such could do unthinkable damage.

Snakes and crocs more or less covered, our briefing cautioned us about some of the other lesser-known dangers here, such as Monitor lizards, tarantulas, and scorpions, whose ordinariness here belies the fact that every nature institute in the world would like to pin a specimen to their boards, so ancient are these Gabonese species. There had been sightings of leopards as close to the camp as to be classified 'on the camp' and, quite shockingly, there are even toxic bees to keep a look out for.

From time to time the place is unusually invaded by a swarm of something or other a little strange in the insect world. Of particular thrill to the camp children and particularly disgusting to adults are the waves of Rhinoceros Beetles that choose to make the Yenzi camp home for a short séjour. Rhino Beetles are amongst the world's largest, deriving their name from the characteristic horns that the males of the species have and are known to be amongst the world's strongest animals in relation to their size. Apparently, on occasion, the nets around our two tennis courts at the club become homes to hundreds of these flying creatures who descend on the place, making their entry unconventionally from across Lake Yenzi. Harmless enough to those who don't mind the tickle of an enormous crusty-backed beetle on their bodies, the Yenzi children cycle to school, taking a beetle clinging to each shoelace along for the ride. We left the presentation a bit more knowledgeable and a lot more scared, pondering the ability of our liberally applied insect repellents actually to protect us from anything much at all.

Despite the danger the wildlife imposed and adhering to strict guidelines that forbids being on foot after twilight due to the elephant hazards, I began jogging, feeling strong enough now in body, mind and spirit to take on comfortably such energetic pursuits. This was a far cry from my earlier running forays, which were a frantic business akin to an excited greyhound being let out of its trap and off in pursuit of its trophy. In my case, rather than any thoughts of what might lie ahead to hearten my stride, I knew I was running away from my own internal turmoil that was impossible to outrun. This adjusting to camp life, without home comforts, the coolness of the welcome from the camp residents and multiple thoughts of past woes and past pain that had been stirred up, had brought me to a deep low. Sometimes I'd quietly sit and wonder if my angels were shaking their heads in despair at me and my ability to be felled emotionally in this way. I was sure that by now and with so many spiritual books and healing sessions under my belt, my skin should have thickened beyond this epidermis of mine that seemed pervious and sensitive to everything.

It seems that a spiritual path is a journey, an unfolding, and one must never consider it as a destination or an arrival at a life of bliss. There are no silver bullets to a quick fix and always lessons and insights to gain, without which life has a futility and empty irrelevance. Times of turmoil, such as these early Gabon days, prompt a little re-group and inward think until clearer understanding is attained, and are part of the process, yielding soul teachings. Nevertheless, lows can move in. This point was enforced during my early runs on the camp, the naïve thought that any woes in my head would somehow be expired along with the sweat out of my pores was symptomatic of a spiritual pulled muscle. My runs, inconsistent and out of pace, shoulders high and body held taught like my mind, were bereft of any calmness, as though each footstep further tightened strings and intensified bindings instead of releasing strain.

Slowly, I'd begun to yield and to acclimatise to my new world. I took the time to reflect within and felt a reassurance descend around me. I considered myself entirely blessed, in fact all of us residents blessed, to be chosen to live in an environment bristling with such a wealth of animal and plant life. Embracing all of that beauty, a growing connection seemed to stir within me and, whilst I wasn't actually punching the air in glee, I began to feel more contented and more grounded than I'd felt for as long as I can remember, with days punctuated with the odd 'perfect moment'.

My jogging had taken a literal new route around the golf course area and seemed to reinforce a oneness I was feeling with the nature around me. In the early days I'd trotted around the camp streets, hurdling the plentiful speed bumps, negotiating the few vehicles and attempting to keep my huffing and puffing to a respectable minimum, aware that the beat of my loud encouraging rock music masked much of my own sounds from my ears. This public route had the added disadvantage of requiring one to save enough air for the many "Bonjours" needed to greet each passing ménagère, all brightly clothed and cheery as they arrived on the camp for their daily duty.

Instead, now I was running alone around the golf club, the prettiest and most peaceful area of the camp. The course is also the highest point, which at this stage of my training I'll call slightly hilly, if not vaguely mountainous at times, especially into the headwind that seems to arrive regularly with the tying of my trainers, suddenly and out of a still sky. The runs begin with a left turn, down Monkey Road and after a short jog, a right into the remoter areas of the camp, past dense jungle on both sides and opening out to a bridge over a river. This area not so many weeks previously was one that I'd found particularly frightening, so much so that it had taken me weeks to pluck up courage to drive through with my car windows down, even a few centimetres. There are constant jungle creaks and cracks and occasional monkeys leaping from branch to branch with an inquisitive eye trained on you, and flattened palm leaves indicating that elephants have traversed, hopefully a safe time ahead, to keep you on your toes.

I feel only mildly anxious running thorough that area now and manage to keep to a minimum the occasional panic. There are often the crashes in the trees to contend with and internal dialogues as to whether it may be an actual live gorilla, which neighbours say have been sighted there. Occasionally, when I'm running past disturbed timber sounds, with mild to moderate gorilla thoughts in my head, I wonder what I'd actually do in the unlikely event that the theoretical were ever to become a reality. I have a somewhat comical picture that springs to mind of a man in gorilla costume chasing me. I realise that the thought of an actual gorilla and I being up there alone, running round the 8th tee box, me with my modesty top tied tight around my Lycra joggers in a respectable '40-plus-years old' way, is too terrifying to conjure up in precise and real detail and that the comedy version is good enough.

I've sometimes chosen not to take my music out on the runs with me, preferring to tune into the sound my feet make as they cross the varied terrain and the general ambient tunes. Things begin with a laterite gravel crunching, as I divert my mind from the steepness of the incline by taking in the little pattern details carved in the gravel, as well as keeping an alert eye for any possible snakes en route. I tell myself how fortunate we are that the bright orange of this African laterite, spread so commonly as road surfaces here, would contrast brilliantly with most, if not all, of the indigenous snakes of Gabon.

As with the elephant tales, there are many snake-linked horror stories to confine you to the interior of your house for the duration of your posting. There are two particular golf course snake tales that spring to mind which add a certain pulse to my pace as I progress round the course. I've heard it told that a jogger-lady doing her thing, not unlike myself, had 'almost' trodden on a venomous Gabon Viper, which had been lying in her path masquerading as a stick, and which at the eleventh hour she had to take jumping avoidance action over. Another gentleman had the misfortune to step on a snake during his workout runs, with the snake jumping to the left and he to the right, neither particularly keen on making acquaintances. It bemuses me that despite contraindications, such as being a terrible insect and particularly snake coward, I find myself enjoying this lone running and deriving an uncharacteristic thrill from the excitement of this bungee jump in nature.

The gravel crunches take you up and around the course, slipping past the 4th hole to the left, and once at the top the view opens out to unfold the magnificence of the Yenzi Lake, around which our camp is built and which I always find a peaceful, serene and heartening sight. The shimmering water is set off against a backdrop of African plains in the distance, with their tapestry of greens and distinguished African trees. Most often I take a few seconds there to inhale the beauty that sits quietly around. It's a view that's on offer to all of us, there for the taking, but not one that screams at you impatiently to look and appreciate as some brash views irritatingly do. Africa is self-deprecating and as with my little leaves sprouting in Edinburgh from cracks, the sight is all the more awesome for its modesty. As a contrast to the Edinburgh plants, however, this scene has a powerful feel to it of longevity, of having been there, looking just so beautiful, growing through its seasons already for so long and onwards to infinity. Somehow it strikes you that this beauty here is so unspoilt that nothing will ever change it, no large housing or hotel developments will arrive to flatten forests and seasons will come and go just as they have always done. There is no sense of history, of buildings being built and re-built, as most of us are accustomed to. Instead, this country seems to keep life to brief present moments.

Gabon is nicknamed the world's last Natural Eden and it's easy to see why. The permanence and power of nature here are like nothing I've felt before. They, along with the vastness of the animal-filled rainforests and miles of empty white beaches, are humbling reminders of one's own small place and small role within it, leaving only our personal tiny tracks after we are gone. We few inhabitants, locals and expatriates alike must consider the honour we have been bestowed for being amongst the select few able to share with such intimacy nature's secrets.

The running route now veers right away from the lake, steering as wide as possible past the crime scene of a former snake incident and up a gentle incline. This time my footsteps pound on a grass track rooted in sand beneath and I try to keep concerns of random swooshing sounds and the band of disturbed grass blades that appear to be disobeying the upright trend and stillness of the rest, to a minimum. I direct all energy to the legs and to speeding up and out of there. Fast. I skip past the 15th, with its faded flag flapping to celebrate my arrival, and rejoin the laterite track leading over the bridge and past the splashes of scurrying wildlife taking to the water fearful of my pounding feet and onto the finish line. Cleansed and refreshed, I'm soon back home, having been a million miles away in my sanctuary.

I often reflect that the camp residential area should have been built up here, with its hilly relief and inspirational views. The present uninspiring company club, restaurant and pool area could have happily spread itself out, creeping along the lower reaches of Lake Yenzi, with the golf course exchanging territory with the houses and plentiful trees, sure to ruin a great fairway shot, in exchange for the awesome view.

The present restaurant taps into none of the amazing potential of such a dynamic setting, with its small windows viewing nondescript sights and completely missing the awe of the lake, viewed only after dinner around a corner and from outside. How stunning a rustic, African-style club would have been, located on the edge of the lake and with a restaurant out on a pier held safe in the calming lake waters. It would have given us a focal point to socialise within nature's embrace and might, I reason, have gone some way to coaxing some of the camp residents from their insular mode, dropping their guards and melting amidst such a splendour and harmony.

We have a pantomime villain-type character overseeing the running of the main club and restaurant areas. A tall, elongated man from Denmark, with steely eyes that squint over the top of the reading glasses he wears at all times and coldly pierce his victims through the heart. He strides across our unassuming and tired jungle patio with a gait more suited to the anxious walk of someone important in a busy international airport and constantly complains about his miserable lot. Every encounter with him is peppered with his moans, including the elephant situation on the camp. He has the misguided notion that he is being personally singled out for particular provocation by these animals and carries two silver torches in his hands at night, to flash in the eyes of the hulking animals to shoo them away from his territory. I can't help thinking that the torches must appear as an extension to his piercing and unfriendly eyes, as though he has plucked the nastiness from his sockets to shine like eyeballs in his lean and wiry hands. I've tried, since arrival here, to engage with him and to find a chink of softness, a subject, or a something that brings some sort of a shine of hope to his miserable face, but have now exhausted all options and keep out of his way instead.

I learned in early days of school Biology classes that in life there are the 'tongue-rollers' and there are 'non-tongue-rollers'. With much more of life's awareness now under my bridge of knowledge than the young girl who was so fascinated by these early biological revelations, I would revise that there are 'glitter sprinklers' and there are 'cloak bearers'. There are the sorts of people who make you feel better for having been in their presence, no matter for how long or in what context the exchange. Some people, living angels perhaps, carry with them a bag of glitter and liberally sprinkle it over every-thing and everyone they encounter. They have no meanness, nor a desire to create limiting rations of amounts of sparkle to be distributed. They know that there will always be enough glitter to go around and that their own reserves will be simultaneously replenished. They cannot help but proffer such a positive hue to exchanges, nor fail to exude such lifting energy.

In stark contrast, there are the cloak bearers, whose presence in a room can be felt as a cloak of darkness, swirling up and around in theatrical style and with the sole purpose of absorbing and concealing any bright lights and sparkle encountered. Dark cloaks are all around, just like our character in Gabon, who is highly ill-suited to a career in the service industry. Dark cloaks are energy drainers, with their pessimistic slant on life and are unsettled and made uncomfortable by those who appear overly cheery.

At all costs, however, glitter sprinklers must clutch their little bag of light and continue to throw their magic around. The light will always triumph in the end and shine out undiminished and remembered. Dark, miserable cloaks will exit stage left and be forgotten, erased from minds of others who refuse to allow such negativity to reside within them.

Chapter 7

Yenzi Camp to the Rescue

A s with my present mental refit of the Gabon camp, I've always had a fixation for redesigning rooms, shops, restaurants and the like, silently changing colour schemes and moving furnishings, whilst sipping coffee and mid-conversation with friends. At times, I've had to remember to focus on my part of conversation and offer my words to the verbal exchange, when the interior refit schemes in my head become powerfully three-dimensional and distracting. I'm also aware that at times a relaxing coffee or lunch with my husband can be somewhat stressed by opinions of ambient improvements, spilling into my head and which I have to release with all my creative enthusiasm. I occasionally sense my husband's unspoken hush, as he stirs his cappuccino froth, trying to distance himself from my excitement, sometimes so overwhelming and urgent that I forget to savour the moment along with my apple-cinnamon muffin, zoning out immersed in my creative thoughts.

This interior passion and vision to see things, places and people rise to their full potential, has been with me from childhood. Coupled with that and for as long as I can remember, I've had an unwavering desire to find a market-niche for a product or service, to earn some pocket money at the very least, if not to generate sweeping riches from an original idea hitting a target.

I often recall what I consider to be my first entrepreneurial venture but which, like many of my schemes, never did have the business plan framework to launch it skywards and into fiscal returns. I'd been fishing in the river that ran parallel to our family home, along with my two sisters and neighbourly friends, when good fortune presented itself. After a quiet half–hour and little success, small minnows began taking up positions in our nylon nets, precariously perched on the end of long bamboo rods and ripped in various places. We'd carefully and excitedly started to deposit our catches into an old coffee jar, barely rinsed and with its label and branding still in evidence along with the lingering aromas of adult drinks.

I remember being overcome with excitement at the prospect that we might be able to boost our pocket money by selling the little fish to the plentiful friendly neighbours in the vicinity. Without further ado, my able team, sensing the wisdom in my plan, packed up rugs, picnic and comics and began knocking on doors, brimming with the confidence a bunch of optimistic and dreamy six-year olds has. We were undaunted by the polite refusals of our first few prospective customers and continued for the remainder of the pre-tea-time hours to try to sell our now slightly murky fish and novelty 'tank'. In retrospect, we should have realised that at least half our targeted market were in their sunset years, eighty if a day and could barely focus on the contents of the jar, never mind be inclined to introduce livestock to their rosewood and lace homes. Undaunted by no exchanges of actual cash, I'd found the entire experience to be a delight from beginning to end. There had been the fun of the catch, participating in a joint pursuit in the heat of warm summer's day, the safety of home never out of sight and spending time with sisters and best friends. There had been the thrill of devising a plot, a money-making project, and finally the unfaltering warmth of the welcome that met us on every doorstep. I think on that day, my entrepreneurial head was fully born.

I contemplate, too, my school days in Edinburgh. Our school took up much of a residential street, spread around various large houses full of old-world character and not one single building too imposing. There was no great dominant façade with turrets and stone gargoyles glaring down to make small children in oversized uniforms feel any smaller they already felt. This was a school we'd moved to in a hurry, when our former one closed down due to lack of funding. Strangely, the previous one had been a magnificent building, set in the heart of beautiful grounds sprinkled with ancient trees that had captivated my imagination. My playtimes were most often spent huddled up at the foot of these great tree trunks, digging and carving out the wonderful buttress roots, before making installations using broken twigs and leaves placed strategically with the precision of a surgeon. I don't recall if the objective was to create Andy Goldsworthy-inspired art, which I adore, or if the idea was to make homes for the dollies and little plastic horses I always carried around with me in my pockets, but at any rate I loved this break-time with a passion. I still never pass a buttress-rooted tree without my mind flashing back to that era and to such simple pleasures, to the joys of a fresh, innocent mind and to my raw and emerging creative shoots beginning to sprout.

Our old school also had an ominous past, having once been an orphanage and there was an out-of-bounds area, which I visited either in an approved or unapproved way, and which held tiny, simple graves randomly set in and around the trees. These, whilst shocking and eerie to such a young and over-imaginative mind, were in no particular order, as one might have expected. Perhaps the sadness of the scene was offset by the notion that the graves had somehow chosen to grow where they wanted out of the yielding soil, nestled at the base of protective oaks or in the loving arms of a matronly holly bush. Considering this history, and the imposing school building with its massive columns, dwarfing even the teachers, I remember the place to have been filled with a positive energy and a pervading happiness.

I recall latter senior school days, in the scattered houses in the quiet Edinburgh street, to have been a general happy affair but not a period which creates any particular stirring on looking back in time. No great horrors and no great pleasures. Some of my strongest memories, apart from my days spent in the Art Department with a most inspirational teacher, were days when the book sales and home-baking events took place. The book sale events were an opportunity for us to sell our old textbooks, preserved neatly in their home-made brown paper covers, and to buy the required reading material for the next academic year. I loved these trading days and particularly to be receiving good cash as a reward for having looked after my school books so carefully during the course of the year. Mindful of the end of year sales, I'd forgone the desire to doodle on the text books when the mind wandered off learning issues and teachers' voices and instead I'd encouraged my pens to freely create their random patterns over my jotters. I remember once buying a mint-condition book from a careful owner which I re-sold after only minutes in my possession. I then purchased a tired, dog-eared version that I reasoned hidden behind a fresh brown cover would look fine and importantly allowed me to generate a small profit.

The home-baking days too, were a time when we were allowed to turn our desks around and out of their usual front-facing regularity and instead to line the perimeter of the room, each displaying our home-made goodies. Little eye-catching signs sat alongside plates piled high with scones and iced fairy cakes, denoting appropriate prices, and a discrete receptacle was hidden under the desk in which to deposit the monetary gains. As a tribute to both parents, I don't recall my sisters and I ever being asked for the proceeds of either of these sales days on our enthusiastic return home. We were allowed to retain the profits along with the feeling that we'd done exceedingly well.

From then on, I always pledged to make the most of an opportunity or of a specific location to indulge my entrepreneurial notions and to grasp opportunities in my reach. There was a time I made and sold earrings and brooches, all painstakingly hand-rolled and baked from a plastic derivative, and all individual in their wealth of colour and pattern. I'd devised a brand name and for a brief sales period the jewellery was sold on hand-decorated cards, embellished with the company logo.

At one point, before children had arrived in the family, my husband and I spent a period of time in London, due to his work commitments. I'd tried to use my resources to sell dried flower wreaths and arrangements that I busied myself making into the wee small hours. I used to take them around shops, in a rather naïve and unstructured, un-business-like way, but remember being overcome with the joy of having some creative handiwork in the public domain. My husband could always be relied on for supportive words, transport and patience with a sometimes chaotic house, crowded with box after box of stock and occasional gold cloud of pervading paint fumes. Over the years, he has turned his hand to stringing up giant polysty-rene snowflakes, being sales assistant and porter at some of my many creative stalls, along with being assistant producer of an African art exhibi-tion in Scotland on behalf of one of my Nigerian artist friends.

London had been an exciting period for me creatively, and my flower work and general bent for interior styling led me to being offered a position in an ultra-stylish flower shop adjacent to Bond Street. I was in Heaven. The shop was incredibly classy and far removed from the minimal chic look that is so 'in' these days. We had splendid windows wrapping around the whole front shop area and an imposing grand entrance. Once inside, there was a somewhat moody, atmospheric tone, with stone floors and benches and wonderful round tables also in stone, from which brilliant bursts of cut stems sprouted out of clear glass containers, arranged strictly according to colour. I was deeply honoured to be employed by such a notable establishment and to join heads with the intoxicating talent.

I was initially a part of the plant department and spent time being trained to make stunning planted baskets and containers for anything from tropical orchid baskets to miniature rose gardens. We had a celebrity clientele and on one occasion, as part of my plant department's remit, I found myself assisting with the planting of bay trees at the entrance to Clarence House. I met the Queen Mother's steward 'Backstairs Billy' and his colleague and was shown around their tiny and modest house. The walls were crammed full of signed photos of members of the royal family and the cramped living room was scattered with small, glazed cabinets, housing a lifetime's enamel box collection.

The shop was managed by an exotic and pencil-thin lady, always dressed impeccably. She'd arrive daily, stepping out of a chauffeur-driven Rolls Royce and float through the premises en route to her office in an adjacent building. She had a warmth about her, yet fastened into her tightly-fitted, tailored suits, an aloofness that could at times be daunting. Nevertheless, her presence had me transfixed and I still remember vividly the scene of her arrival each day, amidst an aroma of perfume that man-aged to make its sweet bouquet heard above and beyond the natural floral fragrances bursting from all corners of the shop.

Captured by the buzz of London and inspired by so many creative heads coming together like this, it wasn't long until I found myself transferred to other areas of the shop and away from my metal bin of compost. I was given the glorious title of 'Colour Co-ordinator' and was delighted to have the stunning shop windows, in their prestigious location, fall under my remit. In those youthful days, creativity flowed as and when it was required and there were never any challenges that caused me sleepless or disturbed nights. On occasions, my windows were filled with beds of heather plants and azaleas in dazzling colours, interspersed by textures. Sometimes I had structures of wire and moss, decked with red apples, extravagant clumps of roses and wheat and I fondly recall a striking Hallowe'en display with the windows full of hundreds of fresh pumpkins, several with dramatic, gothic arrangements sprouting forth. I began to get a feel for the sorts of things that would sell and always derived a great thrill from someone, often a recognised TV or magazine face, stopping their cars to make impromptu purchases from my windows.

In low and unsettled periods, like the first tentative weeks in Gabon, I reflected on the periods of my life and wonder at what point ease and confidence of youth, of unwavering faith in the ability to decorate W1 windows and arrange baskets of sweet peas for Queen Mothers, turned to the fears and self-doubts that unsettle my adult head. My spiritual search has unearthed the notions of the fresh soil of youth becoming strewn with the weeds of criticism and negative feedback, which left to grow take on super roots that have a tendency to penetrate deep. Over time and untended, the plants you chose to sow for yourself in your personal, emotional allotment of creativity, of unconditional love, of faith, have little space to thrive amidst the weed-ridden plantation. A little shift takes place, distorting the vision and values that were once so youthfully clear to you and your inner core crumbles. What is left is an outer shell, at loggerheads with the wonders of subconscious flow, clumsy and contrived and no longer able to tune in to your personal song guiding from within. Everywhere I look, I see people who have forgotten how to dance to the beat of their own music and who would benefit from some emotional weeding and focused cultivation. It's not my business, nor anyone's to intervene, but perhaps a book lent or wise comment passed may inspire some steps in a different direction. A few small steps towards compassion and unconditional love can change the world.

*

One of the favoured African pursuits, particularly over weekends, is to take to the deserted and stunning beaches in Gabon. We have 800 kilometres of unending white sand, lapped by sparkling seas. Occasionally there are night parties involving a chain of 4 x 4s heading off into jungle tracks and cruising over soft treacherous sand towards a faint torch or fire-glow in the distance signifying people and fun. As newcomers, on the way home from such an evening, we'd christened our vehicle, stuck fast and bellied-out in sand so soft you could have bathed in it. There were three of us in the car, my husband and I and another newcomer, or 'fresh fish' as we'd been called in Nigeria. Earlier in the evening we'd congratulated each other on how well we'd managed to pull together rudimentary picnic utensils from bare cupboards and struggling suitcases to equip us for the party. Now however, digging out a very stuck vehicle surrounded by darkness and dense animal-laden jungle, equipped with two teaspoons and a few wine glasses, was going to be a challenge.

Martin, our travelling companion, had taken the precaution of purchasing a machete. Despite the fact that he had only one cup and one saucer and one plate in his company house, the top item on his list for purchase from the local village had been a machete. He was now using it to slice across the bushes, hacking off branches to be put under our wheels like some untrained extra from Pirates of the Caribbean who had forgotten it was a dress rehearsal and turned up in yellow t-shirt and shorts and without the customary jaunty hat. We'd made acquaintance in a police station in Libreville weeks earlier, processing his 'carte de séjour', our residence permit for living in Gabon, along with us. He'd smiled empathetically at the distressed dog sounds leaking out of the company bus as we patiently waited for the slow-paced paperwork to be over and to be reunited with Travis, anxiously awaiting our return in the bus.

When the branches failed to give our vehicle the necessary purchase to enable forward momentum, we turned to Plan B. Next step was to release air from the tyres at the same time as crossing our fingers, hopeful that somehow wider, softer tyres would have the metal beast heaving its belly up and out of its sandy trap. Several failed attempts later and not a moment too soon, we heard a car in the distance and certain rescue. Within minutes four fellow ex-pat bodies dismounted from their vehicle and began instructing each other. It was obvious that they had several incidents of experience beyond us as they prostrated themselves under our car and begun hauling armfuls of sand out, ladies and men alike. We were all instructed to get behind the car and push whilst the driver did his bit with the low gears, and we were quickly briefed as to our specific roles. I remember thinking how incongruous the black Chanel nail polish and beautiful sparkly flip-flops looked on the lady to the left of me and she pushed our car with all her weight behind it; but, a lover of fashion myself, I staunchly applauded her efforts at maintaining her European style out here in the jungle. The banter was fun, the camaraderie and Dunkirk spirit were just what we'd been needing after difficult weeks and an awkwardness from the rest of the residents of the camp. The car, however, refused to budge.

Much later, and with us newcomers trying to banish concerned thoughts rising as to the wildlife that must have by now congregated in the bushes beside us to watch the spectacle of the stuck 4 x 4, further assistance declared its presence in the form of revving engine sounds in the distance. Soon we had four more rescuers to boost the morale and swell the automobile rescue ranks. Again the passengers descended on the scene, familiar with their well-practised support roles and with the military precision of teams I'd only seen previously in the Edinburgh Military Tattoo. Before the guns had sounded and arms had saluted, our synchronised helpers had assumed their positions and had unravelled and stretched a winch from their car to ours.

Embarrassingly, particularly as seasoned sand drivers with more than ten years of Middle Eastern desert driving under our fan belts, we'd done a good job of getting ourselves well stuck. Eventually the winch did the trick and the car hauled itself out shame-faced and limped onto its now entirely deflated tyres. Unable to drive our own vehicle back, we left it in the careful watch of the buffalos on the plains and in the kindest spot we could find for poorly wheels and new tyres deplete of air. We hitched a lift back to the camp, spreading ourselves around the other two vehicles and would return for our abandoned baby in the morning.

I felt strongly that night that our being stuck was the greatest of blessings and that in this way we'd somehow managed to catch both ourselves and our rescuers off-guard and had begun to make friends. It was just possible, after all, that we had created at least some of our own resistance to the new faces encountered and perhaps contributed in some way to the diffused welcome we'd met on the camp.

We subsequently made several off-road bonding trips, very often requiring the assistance of some manpower and shovel digging as well as Martin's skilled machete chopping to set us on our way and each time doing that bit more for the friendship situation. Nature has a way of disarming and stripping inhibitions and permitting warm hands to extend, which we are always very grateful for. I've begun to fall in love with the country, the rugged unspoiled terrain, and to delight in the excitement of picnicking amidst fresh elephant tracks, exotic mangroves and parrots. I'm always transfixed by the sight of the African sun, turning into a huge ball of bright red fire, before dropping into a luminous sea and the moon assuming its position opposite. There can be no more powerful way to remind yourself of the continuity of life and our fleeting moments within it.

There were always plenty of wildlife tales recited to stunned audiences. It didn't seem to matter how long you had spent living in the jungle camp, these stories were able simultaneously to raise eyebrows and awareness. There had recently been a tale of horror encountered on a simple trip to buy diesel from the one small petrol station in the neighbouring village of Gamba. Steph, a robust lady, who'd been on the ex-pat merry-go-round for more years than all of us put together and who also liked her tipple, was waiting for diesel at the fuel station when chaos ensued. A particularly confrontational cobra had decided to investigate the busy fuel station, irrespective of the noise of people and car engines and was headed towards the two pumps. One of the vehicles also queuing for fuel was full of Gabonese locals and, sensing the extreme danger of this reptile, the driver began directing his tyres over it, round and round, dragging it until its skin was horrifically ripped from its body. Loud cheers and claps rang out at the sight of the venomous creature being destroyed. Captured cobras are always killed in Gabon, due to the extreme danger they present. Steph's story wasn't to end there, however, as moments later, still waiting her turn in the small fuel queue, more excited cheers sounded as a troupe of elephants, eight of them including young, wandered through the station. As if one needed a reminder that this was no European service station, with its one elderly diesel pump and rear trouser pocket as a cash desk.

I'd also recently listened shocked to a similar story, whilst doing my shopping in the supermarket on the camp. A neighbour of ours, Sandra, had been on her way home from dropping a child at school and was making the five minute journey home on her bike, when she saw a snake come down her driveway. Bikes are a common mode of transport on the camp for office and social trips and my husband prefers this method of transport on his commute to the office, weather and elephants permitting. He has already had an encounter with a 4 ft luminous green Monitor lizard that seems to stake out the track to the office and is regularly encountered lurking along the route. Sandra watched the snake as it slithered into the flowerbeds in her garden and made her way up the drive, keeping to the farthest edge and as far as possible away from the serpent danger. Suddenly, the snake reared out of its floral hideout and flattened its neck, sending her fleeing inside the house to call for help. Her descriptions of the neck flattening and reared body had raised the highest alert and deployed the emergency response team. Soon vans of men were arriving to catch and kill the reptile, which had now managed to escape somewhere in the vicinity of the house next door. Following a two-day stake-out, the snake was located under the bath of the unwitting occupant. It transpired that there was a cobra nest between the walls of the house and the bath was removed and walls demolished to render the place safe. Each day, when passing Sandra's house, number 44, with its children's swings regularly blowing unoccupied, during my early morning dog walks, I'd raise my own alert status to high, downgrading to amber on making the right turn at the corner of her street.

The food shopping side of the camp life is one that I struggle with, along with the rest of the camp residents. After being spoiled by an unlimited supply of fruit and vegetables in Muscat, I find the dismal and depressing selection here gets to me. Astoundingly for an African country, even bananas are a rare treat. Due to the camp remoteness, the poor quality of the local soil and the damage by rampaging hungry elephants, fruits and vegetables are in short supply. Our company supermarket is stocked mostly by imported goods, flown down here from Libreville in limited quantities. I'd become obsessed by trying to ensure that we always had enough materials in the `fridge at least to make a simple salad. I'd often take myself off to the nearby plantation to try to buy lettuces and tomatoes. Most times I'd leave with a couple of dirty lettuces and three or four tomatoes. Before placing in the `fridge to try to preserve them for as long as possible it was necessary to wash them several times in mild bleach to make sure the elephant dung fertiliser had been removed.

On one occasion I'd asked the French man who ran the shop on the camp if he would reserve a lettuce for me, due to be imported from Holland on the Saturday. He had explained that there was going to be a single lettuce coming and he would put my name down against it. I left the shop shaking my head. A single lettuce seemed a paltry attempt at stocking a food store to supply a camp full of families. Saturday arrived and as soon as I'd spotted the small Dornier `plane fly over our house, I'd headed to the shop to collect my order, only to be told by an apologetic shop manager, in his French-flavoured English, that it had not arrived. It hadn't seemed a lot to ask, but even such a simple food request often failed to be met in this location.

As a result of the poor choice and limited availability, people chose to send air freight shipments once in a while to buffer the miserable local selection. In the camp store, it seems as if the entire shop is brimming with large, catering sized tins of soggy peas, beans and vegetables. I find we've had to make sweeping changes to our normal diet, which used to consist of plenty of stir-fried crunchy vegetables. Stir-fries are very much off the menu here due to a lack of green or crunchy things to fry and instead we have to do our best with a frozen selection, boosted by vitamin tablets. Believing that an army marches on its stomach, it shocks me that a large, international family company should not give more priority to bringing fresh food for us all. Some of us, depending on flight availability, will make an overnight trip to Libreville, armed with cool boxes and ice packs, later returning with luxuries such as cheese and dairy products, chunks of meat and vegetables. In Gabon I never discard food. In the case of something like a half tomato, if only part is required, then the already over-ripe balance is carefully stored in the `fridge for later. Despite one's own sense of lack and frustrations at the inability to buy any nutritional quality or variety here, you can't help but reflect on those less fortunate, never many feet away from you and often with no running water or electricity. It is most likely that few of us westerners have ever had our food selection as restricted as it is here and it gives us a small taster of what life must be like for the many people around the globe who would consider our limited Yenzi shop food to be extraordinarily special.

Many of the men on the camp spend weekends fishing, enjoying the world-class quality of the beach fishing in this area. A line cast into the sea here can yield a fish of 40 kilos and more and, importantly, bolster many a gasping freezer. A sand and jungle drive, where occasionally gorillas are spotted, culminates in a final jungle push or 'scratchy tunnel' as it's affectionately known, and onto stunning open sea views. I've never seen car bodywork damaged quite like the scars on car paintwork that these jagged tunnels of thorn trees inflict, akin to giving a car a wash with a pan scourer instead of a sponge. The gouges in car manufacturer's paintwork eventually fill with orange laterite and the vehicles take on a distinctive striped livery. A white car such as ours is particularly vulnerable to this orange discoloration.

Life in the jungle was becoming a bit less strange and even without the arrival of our main container sent from Oman, a small shipment had arrived from Edinburgh with the spinach soup paint, which we'd taken no time in applying to appreciative walls. The colour suited the jungle environs to perfection and added a bold, personal statement to the uniformity of the company accommodation, but had darkened the room considerably, making the task of evening reading almost impossible. The golf, runs and tennis were keeping me in exercise contentment and I was relishing my meditation, chill times surrounded by birdsong. In addition, my painting was flowing onto canvas with a new depth and energy. Travis too was taking to his new surroundings and had begun to relax into the place. He had taken particular delight in meeting the many new faces, human and doggy alike, and had formed a special bond with a little Maltese lady friend. At any opportunity she would slip from her home confines and bound down the small hill intent on sneaking into our house to meet her boyfriend. The excited pair would then begin jumping on and over every piece of furniture in their delight at securing a rendezvous.

❈

I thought I'd been doing a good enough job of coping, dealing simultaneously with the past and present emotional difficulties and then it hit: pain,
trauma, a thunderbolt from the sky and a sense of just not being able to
keep on keeping on. We'd been at a Friday club night, a Gabon social
evening open to all families, where we dine on mediocre food whilst seated
around the club patio keeping out of the way from our camp villain. Most
importantly, we'd go there to interact with each other and to keep the
bonding momentum going. Despite the fact that there might often only be
a handful of people show up and the experience had a depressingly apa-
thetic feel to it, my husband and I had wanted to make an effort to leave
our house and support the occasion.

On this particular evening, towards the end, just as we were about to
make our departure, a fleeting comment injected into the air hit me like a
wall of pain. It was a jest, light-hearted banter made by one of the young
company engineers, but it hit me painfully. She suggested as she walked
past our table of four that the two middle-aged married men including
my husband should "hit the town" along with her to go dancing and
return at, say, five in the morning. The town of Gamba consists of some
rustic buildings scattered in the villages, twenty minutes drive away from
our camp, which are notorious for the local ladies, gyrating their African
curves in the local dingy discos. These clubs were all tiny and intercon-
nected by basic footpaths of sand and often had several locals slumped in
areas, high on the hallucinogenic tree roots or just plain drunk. It certainly wasn't my idea of a place to visit and the whole thing had a seedy,
prostitution side to it with so many young girls intent on catching the eye
of a foreign man or two with the possibility of elevating their financial
status considerably.

Her suggestion might have been healthy and harmless enough perhaps
if I'd been one half of a young and in love couple; but young love had long
since left the now fragile union between my husband and I, and I wanted to
stand on my chair and let my scream out for once. I wanted my voice to
resound shockingly off the metal rooftops and clatter to the ground to a
stunned audience. Instead, like I'd been doing for years, I sat and gulped
my screams politely down, dumbstruck, whilst the joke darted round the
table, gathering pace, as these things do particularly in middle-aged com-
munities such as ours.

Whilst the others took up the 'joke' flattered by the suggestion, my teeth bit lips that I'd fixed into a tortured wince. She couldn't have known the torment she was stirring, a twenty-something Dutch engineer and colleague of my husband. Even so, I resented the way she'd excitedly and keenly steered the conversation, enthusiastically whipping up male egos, and the lack of regard she'd shown to us wives, myself and another lady sitting there. I wanted to explain my grimace and the absence of my laughter. Above all, I wanted to tell her that a 'trailing spouse' wasn't my own definition of myself and that I felt I had a vital creative role to fulfil in my life, that soars high above any company indicator code and job title etched on an office door plaque. I wanted to tell her how blessed I feel to be the mother of two amazing boys and, on top of that, to have been granted my artistic talents. She could have no idea how much happiness I derive from my capacity to arrange colour and shape on canvas, harmlessly in my own world and privately expressing what needs to be expressed. Instead, as in all the other incidents of this nature, perhaps for my entire life, I sat silent, wounded most of all by my own decision to swallow pains and humiliation down without offering up any resistance.

As usual, I came home from the experience emotionally stirred and with a growing sense that I had to make changes to my life as thoughts flashed back to previous postings and to my total exhaustion of having this burden shadowing me. But how and when to wave my defeated white flag and how many lives do I devastate in the process of saving one dying soul? In one fell swoop, wounds had opened, exposed again to the emotional elements, stinging in the air and scratched by innocent conversations. I found myself transported, like some cartoon character with superpowers, back in time to six years previously when life had taken an abrupt diversion. I still had issues to resolve and sores to mend. I knew full well that this had to be done, before life would pass with any smoothness and before I could soar to the heights I was intended for. I longed to cut the shackles of this period finally and to be free again.

Chapter 8

Spanish Lessons and Evacuations

The following day, my mind, still six years back in time, churned over events. "I got the job," my husband had told me excitedly. "As usual, they want me to start as soon as possible". I'd been with him in the room while he had his telephone interview via a Nigeria to Amsterdam link-up. His future boss had invited him to Holland for two days for a follow-up face-to-face second interview.

And so, after family discussions we began weighing up the pros and cons of being posted across the Atlantic to South America. My husband seemingly passed the face-to-face interview and accepted his new and promoted position. We left Nigeria with a half-empty container, after selling the bulk of our house contents to willing camp residents there, unable to buy such European choice. Such was the demand for these locally unavailable items that at one point we'd had three eager DIY-ers biting nails in the living room while the earlier bird was making decisions on the contents of my husband's tool box in the kitchen. Due to the differences in voltage there was going to be in the next location, we'd also decided to sell all our electrical kitchen goods, even our trusty ice cream maker which had churned and frozen a delicious pot of vanilla ice every Friday, without failure or complaint.

The formalities for visas for this location required us to attend the country's London embassy in person and present our passports for elaborate hologram stamping. We began our course of specific injections needed for protection in this new location. Meningitis was a must, like the Yellow Fever stipulations for Gabon, which require vaccination certificates to be handed over along with a passport, or sometimes in preference to passports, on every arrival through Customs here.

Some three months after telephone interviews and excited map searches to locate our new home, my husband and I arrived in a Spanish speaking country with one single word of Spanish between us, but clutching a dictionary and enough enthusiasm to master this new language.

Almost from the minute my weary feet touched down from 'plane steps, heavy from months of the usual pre-preparation exhaustion, I'd sensed a pervading and ominous presence in our new country and a feeling of myself as some sort of square peg that would never fit into the place. We were, as is customary, housed in a hotel for the first few weeks until we managed to negotiate ourselves a flat to rent. The hotel, marble-lobbied and grand, gave no indications that the bedroom accommodation would be less than the standard we'd grown to tolerate in Lagos, Nigeria, where I'd learned to carry in my suitcase my own plug to ensure a bath in the orange tap water on arrival.

The room was shocking, easily the worst hotel room I've stayed in and we spent the first night awake listening to the heavy breathing of the occupants in the neighbouring room, whose open ceiling adjoined our open ceiling and blocked nothing. We were both distraught and both regretting our acceptance of such a posting, especially on the back of five years hardship in Nigeria. It seemed we'd bitten off too much.

Whilst my husband initially floundered, I was the one who rallied to the occasion prettying up the room as best I could, with throws and scarves I always carry, and burning aromatherapy essences to soften the blow of the ambiance and try to create a positive mood. From our miserable base and with little or no company support, armed with our Spanish-English dictionary, we began to make appointments to view apartments to rent.

One of my husband's new colleagues, a Norwegian, divorced and remarried to a young local girl and with a newly-arrived baby son, paid us a hotel visit. On his departure his words lingered in my head. "It's not a matter of IF someone from the company gets kidnapped, but WHEN," he said matter of fact. My thoughts had raced home to our two boys in the safety of their boarding school and to our foolishness at having taken on such a risky location. I was shocked and angry for not being made fully aware of the security situation by the company; no specific official line had been offered regards this scenario, almost as though at any cost it was more important to get jobs filled.

We were to go into the office to have kidnap profiles taken the next morning and found the possibility of a restful night's sleep and recovery from our exhaustion slipping even further from our grasp. Thoughts also began to accumulate in my head, like storm clouds amassing and ringing alarm bells at what seemed like a high number of expatriate men now married, or re-married to young local girls.

Morning arrived after more disturbed night-time hours and we took the company chauffeured vehicle the short, hectic trip to the office building. Traffic in this place was like nothing we'd encountered before, with chaos and every man for himself reigning supreme over traffic lights and orderly queuing. We'd assumed on making our decision to move to this location that after Nigeria, nothing could be worse, but this chaotic traffic and the ruthless nature of it seemed even more dangerous than our Nigerian go-slows. The place had a chill to it and there was a palpable aggression that we'd not experienced in Africa. We were in a country surrounded by armed police with their guns to the ready, fingers on triggers and a far cry from the jaunty relaxed guns in Nigeria, with their elastic bands stored on the barrels and swinging like accessories from shoulders.

The office occupied several floors of a modern-looking building and more storm clouds gathered in my head on learning that nobody was aware of my husband's married status or, moreover, that he was actually going to be accompanied by a wife. This thought swilled around between my ears whilst I took in details of the office attire. The dress code was more the sort of thing one would associate with discos and dancing, rather than keyboards and office paraphernalia. Boob tubes barely contained silicon chests and ladies appeared to be either poured into trousers tight enough to reveal bikini lines, or skirts slit to the thigh. And they were everywhere, crawling from cupboards and climbing out of drawers and several times outnumbering the men. Slightly perturbed at the sights and the uneven balance of Mars and Venus, I queued amidst the lovelies, swishing their manes and posing for their kidnap mug shots, as though it was Mario Testino himself behind the lens.

Eventually my turn came and I stepped up to the hot seat, my self-conscious photograph persona even less likely to relax into pose in such an intimidating atmosphere. To make matters worse I was unable to understand or speak a word of the language being tossed around along with the curled locks. Full length photos were required… this way… that way… bad sides and worse sides until there was enough record of my trembling 5 feet 2 inch body should the unlikely and unfortunate kidnapping happen. After the photos, I had to give samples of handwriting, copying out paragraphs of Spanish text and finally giving ideas of the types of literature I read to somehow test authenticity of a future ransom call.

I returned to my hotel room/shrine and to regroup from the distress of the situation and somehow try to come to terms with the idea that I'd not gone spaceward to another planet and that this scary and unwelcoming place was only a transatlantic jaunt from my familiar things, our lovely boys and my own culture.

Eventually, after apartment viewings, challenged by language issues and eliminating a series of dilapidated apartments, we settled on a lesser of evils and a newly-built place overlooking water, but on the thirteenth floor. I hated it. The flat went against all that I hold dear, enclosed and sterile and not even a waving branch interrupting window views to remind you of your connection to nature. The only way when seated to see anything but sky at the tops of windows was to sit on a dining chair on a small area of elevated floor. The flat was entered via a lift that deposited us directly into the living room and which seemed to churn endlessly announcing the arrivals and departures of the other sixteen floors of inhabitants in the block, day and night. Day by day, my husband began to blossom in equal measure to the depression that now held me in its grip. I loathed this place, the unfriendly people, the lack of company support and I was miserable in this bare turret of a home.

My husband had arrived to a warm reception and a glazed office, with plaque, declaring his managerial status to the room containing his large team. Our situations couldn't have been more different. I'd spend my days stuck in the bare apartment, not a knock at the door nor invitation for coffee, not an anything and no vehicle to even try to forge some independence. To add insult to injury, the country was teetering on the edge of escalating civil unrest and the security situation rapidly deteriorating. Our container of goods had been diverted to Panama indefinitely due to the gravity of the security decline and we put any ideas of investing in a car on hold. By now, the offer of a company loan car had expired and we were now reliant on taxis, hailed by `phone after frustrating language exchanges and invisible gesticulations on our side attempting to make ourselves and our restricted grasp of Spanish language understood.

Occasionally luck would be in our favour and a taxi driver with limited English would arrive. Fascinating slants to the security of the place could be gleaned this way. It became clear that the dangers were high in the crowded streets and alleys and that a left turn at the wrong road could have you in a high-risk zone. In our locality we were only a couple of streets away from danger, if one veered off track. The country was plagued by political tensions and drug-related issues and I grew more alarmed at the lack of safety advice from the company and felt that we were unnecessarily being exposed to dangers, without any official guidelines. I felt let down by a company I'd always trusted.

As if to illustrate my point, my husband came home one evening and sat in front of his laptop with a CD he'd brought back from the office. It transpired that this was our company's 'safe driving course' and according to company policy he was now in the throes of taking his course. I thought the effort was laughable on the part of the company and wondered if the swimming test due to take place the following day involve sitting in goggles, trunks and fins in front of a computer screen.

We began to have Spanish lessons, taught by a young girl who came to the flat. As I zoned-out watching only her lips moving and hearing no sound, my head buzzed with the knowledge gleaned hours earlier that one of the company employees had been so taken with his Spanish teacher that he'd sent his wife of 18 years packing, along with the family, and was now married to the Spanish Ms. Coming back abruptly to the room and to the lesson I tuned in again to hear our professor spout in Spanish "He is engineer," indicating my husband, and "You," she luxuriated, "you are housewife." With a toss of her hair she then proceeded to flutter her eyelids and gush, "My eyes are brown." I was furious with such audacity, and desperate to bundle her and her fluttering brown eyes into the lift and push the 'ground floor express'. I wished never to see her again, but just as my humiliation years later on a low-key club evening in Gabon, with fury lapping at my feet, I sat politely and waited for my pulse to settle and my breathing to calm and the lesson to be over.

Everything was falling into place. We'd arrived to a boys' club. It seemed that too many company officials had either traded in their marriages, their old partners in their old shoes, for young stilettoed office girls, brought up from a young age to value the merits of plastic surgery and educated in the art of man-pleasing, or many just had their cake and ate it. Nature in this country appeared to have granted all the women slim lines and good features and cast the men in the mould of Super Mario, with their small boxy frames and thick features. It was no surprise that the ex-pat men and their well-paid international careers were sought after. No hairline was too receded and no girth too full to appeal to someone or other of the opposite sex.

Eventually, after weeks of solitude in the apartment, I was asked out to a leaving coffee morning. I would have exchanged places with the departing lady in a heartbeat. I was cautioned by each lady I met not to leave my man here for one minute on his own due to the predatory nature of the local women, and came home to my turret even more deflated. It transpired that the small 'phone list of ex-pat families was tainted by as much as 70% by this local-lady phenomenon. It became alarmingly obvious that wives were superfluous to requirements and perhaps our presence even created an awkward conflict of consciousness. I missed our two boys and our Nigerian extended family, in a way that felt like actual pain. To have lived as a valued community member, appreciated for what you could offer to the place as well as benefit from the kindness of others, was at polar opposites to serving my sentence in this dreadful place, unappreciated, unexpected and unwelcomed.

Daily, the security issues deteriorated and the sound of sirens and an occasional bomb filled the air. We watched the local TV, in Spanish, with our dictionary to hand, heard mention of fuel running out, and decide to get ourselves out of the place. Our boys were due to arrive within the next couple of days for a short holiday and by the sounds of things the aviation fuel was running so low there was uncertainty as to whether we would be able to leave or not if we delayed. My husband presented our evacuation plan to a company representative, a French man who would also be leaving, but not in any emergency; he was leaving to be married to a young accountant, aged 27 to his 56. As more pieces of this jigsaw of a place came together and the prevalent and predatory nature of this local culture clarified, it crossed my mind that security issues had probably not been at the top of lists when we'd been given the low-down on the merits of the location months earlier.

So, amidst the rising tensions and dissipated excitement of new languages and new lives, we began to pack our evacuation bags, as much as we could carry, and headed to the airport. Often it seems that it's not the falling that hurts but the landing, and we arrived in our Caribbean resort, the nearest evacuation place, shocked and exhausted. Still no official company advice was being offered and we made arrangements to stay for some days, to give our boys, freshly arrived from the UK, some time to recover from the long flight from the UK. The company's London office had expressed concerns at the prospect of sending out two juniors amidst the political unrest and in the end they, miles away from the action, were the ones who showed a better understanding of the situation.

Official advice came from the local division, eventually, in the form now of "Take a holiday out of the country and we'll see how things go." Eventually we managed to get our traumatised family back to the UK on busy flights, two days ahead of Christmas, and we arrived to a winter wonderland of frost and snow and trying to come to terms with the events of the previous eighteen weeks. Reeling from the notion that the dream posting had turned sour at such an early stage, my husband and I scoured any information pertaining to the political crisis and sat it out in the UK. Eventually, Christmas festivities ceased, decked halls had their holly branches removed and, as one year turned to the next, we were unsure what lay ahead.

After a month at home, my husband got word from the company that an office would temporarily be set up in Houston and that he was to show up for duty. Wives, at this stage, could not be accommodated and the situation in our new host country was still far too volatile for any thoughts of a return. And so at this period in my life, desolate and reeling from these emotional storms and missing my old Nigeria days I began my spiritual search.

My husband and I had taken a joint decision that our new posting, with its political turmoil and security issues, was untenable, especially as parents to two young boys, and as such he had requested a transfer. Somewhere in the proceedings, he began to attribute the decision to transfer location singularly to me instead of the 50-50 decision I understood it had been. As he relayed our feelings to his boss, apparently declaring that his wife had "put her foot down", my heart sank. I knew from that minute onwards that chills would remain hanging in the air long after the winter thaws in Scotland made way for spring shoots.

Our long-distance calls between Scotland and South America became more and more icy and the coolness continued to drive a wedge between us. My husband, now mobilized back to a healing city cleaning up after weeks of chaos, and to a bare thirteenth floor apartment, began to thrive. Almost daily, tensions between us escalated to a level that we were barely on speaking terms. He was resentful of family obligations that would pull him away from a posting and a capable workforce he was relishing, and I was in limbo in the UK waiting for any word that a new job had been located and on stand-by to travel. Suffice to say, after several weeks of this impasse, school holidays loomed large and the decision was made that the boys and I should travel back over the Atlantic and spend a month there until the situation clarified.

We arrived in South America to be met by a stranger, to a man with coolness in his eyes and guilt etched in his furrowed brows. The shock of seeing someone I'd known for almost twenty years, a kind and gentle family man, transformed in such a negative way was beyond comprehension. I'd always seen him as a person who was sure of himself and very much 'his own man', and to see him in this confused state, using phrases and mannerisms that were not his own, made me recoil. Nothing I could say made any difference to the situation; my words were impenetrable to his closed-down ears. He'd even taken to listening to Spanish songs in his hired car. I've never felt so rejected, nor so low and protective over our lost boys in the midst of our adult meltdowns.

Finally, I met an angel in the form of a Canadian girl who lived three floors down in our apartment building. A number of sirens were ringing in her head and, with several years of experience in the country, she cautioned me to get the removers in to pack up the few belongings we'd unboxed and to get the family out of there. And fast. She spoke with a wisdom beyond her 25 years and to this day I am grateful to her. My husband's replacement was already in his seat and there was no reason for the nightmare and limbo continuing. Even so, I knew he was in no mood to leave and had been digging his heels in to remain in this land of sugar as long as he humanly could; and so, with a now furious and unsupportive man, and me appearing by default to assume the role of the Wicked Witch, the removers came in and carried our boxes one by one back out of the bare marbled apartment on the thirteenth floor, along with all our hopes and dreams for a happy and healthy posting.

I've never been so relieved to hear `plane wheels click up into the belly of a fuselage as I was on that occasion. As if to demonstrate the damage to marital relations, my husband sat staunchly in his upgraded first class seat and our eldest son, legs longer than mine, sat next to him in my seat. During the flight I struggled to try to keep my brave face on, sitting in such close proximity to our youngest son, who had had a thoroughly miserable time on his transatlantic holiday. A glass of champagne was sent back down the fuselage in the safe hands of a stewardess for my consumption, and I fought my inclination to get up and calmly stride the length of the aisle and pour it over my husband's head. As seems to frustratingly be my way, and not wanting to create a fuss, I left the glass with its happy bubbles rising to the surface in steady streams on my table to be removed, un-touched, later by the same stewardess.

❋

It perturbs me now, taking myself back to these nightmarish events and to this latest humiliation at the hands of this company engineer in Gabon, that what goes through my head is not what is acted out in my body or in my words. The big fight back, the verbal lambasting that seems to bristle from every cell of me, is put on hold and politely controlled and instead of instant retaliation and self-defence I might spend weeks, months or per-haps years resolving the unresolved and bringing myself back up from the depths of such an esteem crash.

I question myself and my quiet demeanour and wonder what it is that makes people react so differently to the same provocations. Try as I might, the instant reaction thing - the great show of emotion - is not my forte. Instead, I vent my turbulence as well as singing my joys in my creative ways. I will weep a million tears on the shoulder of my dear friend, a feisty colourful redhead, with years of ex-pat wisdom under her designer belts and a particular skill for this type of coaching, but I am not a lover of acting out a public drama.

Chapter 9

The Healing Power of the Sea and Creativity

At times, when life seems to spiral uncontrollably downwards, I crave being near the sea, supported in sparkling water, as though cradled safely in God's own hands and sometimes I derive a comfort and security from that in lieu of human embraces in my life. Despite the disastrous state of relations between my husband and I by the time we left South America, we'd opted to continue the ex-pat trail together and he secured a position in Oman. This was to be our second stay in this delightful Middle Eastern country. Coming on the heels of my emotional, spiritual and marital meltdown, the posting was made softer by our decision to purchase a small boat. Initially the idea was that we'd share expenses with another family and in a more frugal way be able to split equally all berthing, fuel and repair costs. In the event our partnership lasted a mere twelve weeks when the family emigrated to Australia and we were left in sole ownership of a shiny new 25 ft boat with two gleaming engines supported on the back. We dutifully christened her Saluki. Salukis are one of the oldest domesticated dogs, with a history dating back to 7000 BC. The breed held the title of Royal Dogs of Egypt and had a distinguished place in an Egyptian household, often mummified with their masters. We'd felt that the unique pedigree and grace of these dogs made the name a perfect match for our boat.

Names and registration details, painted in English and Arabic, on the port and starboard of the boats in the marina berthed alongside ours, were the only things ever to give clues as to ownership. Amidst a sea of uniform white, regular form and requisite buoys, tied strategically to provide some protection from novice mooring skills, it was hard to glean personality types of the individual owners and I used to pay attention to the boat names and try to piece together a profile. I always smiled slipping past Lazy Dayz or the bold and beautiful Mama Mia but felt our name reflected our more understated leaning. Our boat name probably gave no indication either of a happiness level, in the way that Lazy Dayz conjured up a vessel full of partying or happy revellers. Saluki was thankfully quite silent in that descriptive sense. No-one could really tell which end of the happiness or partying scale we lay.

My happiest Oman moments, beyond my creative pursuits and my beloved painting, were times spent cruising on calm seas and taking in the stunningly rugged Oman coastline. My husband and I ventured out every week, occasionally with Travis, to chill in a sheltered bay or inlet. Even those happy hours, however, were never free and unburdened and very often, especially in the first couple of years, when home life was so strained and wounds so raw, tears would run down silently from behind my sunglasses as the boat slipped through the turquoise waters. I find times spent at sea to be incredibly emotional, with the closeness one feels to nature and to the exceedingly beautiful views 360 degrees around. My eyes would dart from the mirrored reflections in regularly calm water, to our progress defined by our wake, to a lone bird overhead tracking our path and to the horizon and the sense that there is always a horizon to aim for, no matter if all hope feels lost.

Frequently, our trips would be blessed with us crossing paths with schools of swimming dolphins and the joy of that sight would never cease to fill me up with delight. To be in water so clear you could see the fluid bodies of dolphins weaving in and out in the wake of your boat is one of the undocumented wonders of the world.

On occasions, calm seas would out of nowhere stir to galloping white horses and we'd have to implement my husband's formidable boat handling skills to negotiate the white tops and get ourselves back to the safety of the marina. I always believe the sea to be all the more magical for its ability to transform from a mirror to a tempest when least expected. Ship maintenance and GPS gadgetry pale into frightening insignificance when a boat is being tossed around in a raging sea. At such times, I'd often find myself contemplating the poor souls who must have perished the world over in their own such maritime disasters. The closer present reality however on our boat trips indicated that the storm clouds hovering above my head and dimming the light were not someone else's clouds, but my own to deal with.

I'd often consider how much energy can be expended by following a course and a compass reading with no regard to the pervading situation, currents, winds or turbulent oceans. I've been at the helm at times and fought furiously to maintain a precise navigational direction, fastidiously taking in the details on the little globe-like compass, swirling and swishing in its liquid dome. I think, much as in life, a little of going with the flow is the best measure to adopt, allowing oneself to be buffeted and shifted off course once in a while instead of at all costs, and with an unrewarded energy expenditure, attempting to adhere to rigid plans. As I often found at sea, easing up on the forward focus did not prevent the trip from concluding, particularly in such tranquil waters as offshore Muscat. Surprisingly, on slackening a grip on the steering wheel, we'd almost always terminate in the general direction intended and small deviations could yield unexpected bonuses such as a shoal of dolphins or the acrobatic flip of a sting ray, leaping from the sea to the sky and returning magnificently into the water.

We considered ourselves to be very fortunate as boat owners and with such unspoilt beauty at our fingertips, but the pervading emotional residue still hanging thick in the air tainted the bliss of these privileged boat moments. On my part, I think the emotions stirred by the surrounding beauty contrasted too painfully and graphically with the disharmony between my husband and me. No money or fortune in the world can mend broken human emotions, only smooth the jags from the edges perhaps and in that sense I felt grateful we had this chance to spend time on the water. It seemed with incredible irony that the more pleasurable our pursuits, the more the relationship between us was exposed to scrutiny and the more my heart longed to be in the company of a kindred spirit who could appreciate my quiet light instead of recoiling from it.

We'd both breathed sighs of relief when our two boys came out to stay with us over boarding school holidays and when any notion of 'romantic' boat trips could be put aside to make way for blow-up tubes, fishing and adventure. The boys always made the most of their break from Scottish chills and provided us with some energetic and fun-filled days out on the sea. It was a relief that despite our pains we were able to unite as a family like this and have genuine family fun.

I'd managed to keep myself busy in Oman despite not being accompanied by the boys and, intent on regaining some self-respect, had turned my hand to what I do best and to creative ventures, particularly painting. I also regularly helped out at one of the local flower shops, often spending days busy on location. I recall one particular project that took our team of fourteen florists four full days of arranging, thirteen hours non-stop each day without breaks. Initially we worked on the family garden, transforming the place into a magical land of burgundy and gold, along with arches swaged with foliage and flowers. We worked in one of the outbuildings which with its marble floors, hand-painted columns and crystal chandeliers was the most magnificent garage I'd ever seen. The main house was a grand palatial type building, pure white and adorned with Middle Eastern architecture, arches and wonderful opulent domes.

Very often, the floral department, with its branches and flamboyant candelabras, had a tendency to spread out beyond its allocated working area and had to be pruned back from time to time when invasions threatened other territories. On this occasion we were inconveniencing the chocolate specialists, who'd been flown in from the Lebanon along with their handmade chocolates and fresh nuts. The chocolate team spent hours painstakingly filling hundreds of gold bowls with their delicious treats. Around the garden, lighting teams from Australia worked their brilliance and targeted specific walls and stuccoed surfaces to bathe in dramatic coloured lights.

The remaining two days were spent on a farm to the west of the city, frantically snipping and chopping handfuls of flowers at a time to complete the necessary arrangements ahead of the bride's arrival and to ensure that the scene would be befitting a princess. A staged area had been built, with a peculiar central globe representing the world, perched on eight pillars and which was to be raised and lowered at relevant moments during the ceremony. The bride would sit beneath this. The wedding, decorated in all-white roses, mirrors and silver crystals would be attended by only the women, six hundred of them. Even with the few elegant local ladies present as we were constructing the décor, like ants working in unison and sweltering under a blistering sun, the air was already heady with the intoxicating aromas of bakhoor, a perfumed wood which was burned to release pungent aromas and used to infuse clothing with its scent. The Middle East, and Oman in particular as the home of frankincense, will always be synonymous to me with its perfumes and natural wonderful scents, distinctly perfuming men and women alike, and for the generous and warm hospitality we were extended on every day of our cumulative nine years there. The place has a warmth of spirit that always made me feel at home, despite geographical indications to the contrary.

With no school runs and after school activity taxi services to provide, I had plenty of time on my hands and I used to take on small decorative projects, including producing the scenery for a fashion show, for which I'd hired thirty car sections. No sooner had I been asked to lend my creative juices than I'd begun to conjure up a pictorial image in my head that would provide an edgy and unusual backdrop. Following much negotiation and discounting of rates expensive enough to have hired a proper car with an actual engine and chauffeur, instead of mere bits of old scrap and chopped in half chassis, I managed to rent the car sections and get them delivered to the venue.

I'd designed and painted a backdrop of a New Orleans street scene, complete with some graffiti, denoting the designer brands represented in the show, and the cars were to be stacked on top of each other, hoisted high thanks to the kindly donation of a crane and positioned to tower on either side of the stage. The two largest car sections were given glorious prominence in each of the front stage sections and had been electrified so that their headlights would be able to beam out signals as appropriate during the course of the event. The scene was further brought to life with metal dustbins, a streetlamp shining from a green metal ornate post, and stacks of tyres as props. The painted wooden scenery and many times recycled cars sprung to life when the music began and PVC-kilted young men sashayed down the catwalk, with more than enough attitude amongst them to complement my gritty backdrop.

On one occasion I was asked, just ten days ahead of Christmas, to come up with a festive Christmas tree to deck one of the shopping malls. Again, as briefs were being discussed with the mall manager and his assistant, my head was already forming images and ideas to fit the bill and my creative pulse speeding up to the pace of a steady jog at the notion of a tree made of metal poles and great sails of silk, in different colours and angles forming large triangular 'branches'. Due to similar defined and rigid opinions about what I deem to be the optimal scheme, and the same rigidity that permits me from moving even one single cushion once an interior has been carefully completed, my ideas once formed in my head take no budging.

And so, I found myself in a metal workshop with my sketches and samples of fabric tying my best to explain my idea to a very enthusiastic but highly bemused Indian workforce in a hot, outdoor workshop in one of Muscat's backstreets. This was a rabbit warren area of town where most things could be bought and almost anything could be mended. Machines, well past their working sell-by dates, and cars that in European countries would have been put to scrap metal sleep, are able to be fixed here for relatively low exchange of cash.

To their credit, and perhaps somewhat to my stubborn Capricorn persistence, we arrived at the decision to make a prototype to be ready for my inspection in two days time. In the meantime I stretched my O grade Maths to the best of my numerical ability, to calculate precisely (or roughly) how much fabric it would take to form my 7 x 40 ft sails, all to be lined in silver lame and all to look wonderful on my iconic tree. I had the grateful co-operation of the manager of a small fabric shop, a favourite of mine, nestled in amongst the many hundreds of similar shops in the fabric market, or souk. I always considered his material selection to be a cut above the competition, with a myriad of colours and degrees of shimmer and fabric weight that beat the rest hands down. The walls of his shop were entirely filled with row after row of rolls of fabric, on end, sticking out of boxes and tempting even the uninspired to reach into their creative pool of inspiration. There wasn't sufficient material on the premises for such an unexpectedly large request, but in time for the inspection of the tree prototype the balance of my order would be dispatched from Dubai.

I couldn't have asked for more assistance and for a service, as ever in these parts, that was fitting for royalty. I'd most likely and shamefully just presented an order which in monetary terms would have taken the store manager months to earn, but the proceedings passed in a highly dignified manner and with a veritable fuss being made over me. There was regularly much concern that a western lady would have to actually stand in any of these shops and it was quite the custom for a dilapidated and well worn chair to be made available to rest weary European bones on. I tended to decline this element of pampering where possible, so long as it seemed I wasn't offending anyone by leaving the little throne sitting in the middle of the shop without a queen.

Eventually, two days of anticipation over, the prototype was ready and from beneath a sheet of satin, and with a magician-like flurry that would normally precede the arrival of a shocked bunny in a hat, all was revealed. The buzz in the room was palpable and the excitement at having so speedily transformed my strange request into miniature 3-D reality. A hush descended on the grubby workshop and twenty pairs of expectant eyes, most in need of a good rest, bath and decent food, awaited my verdict. I gave the signal to go ahead and was reassured a hundred times by the workshop manager that my tree would be delivered to its festive spot in the mall in seven days time.

Meanwhile, I co-ordinated with a company who were going to shine cascading snowflakes onto the sails of my tree, using some animated stencils and hopefully create a buzz of excitement, especially for children spending Christmas in such an unseasonably warm location. During the construction period, I made repeated visits to the workshop to check the progress of the tree. I'd always head home on each occasion only mildly reassured by the many twisted lengths of metal, lying across the litter-strewn floor and the gushing reassurances that the deadline would absolutely not be exceeded.

Tensions began to rise slowly as the day drew nearer and still nothing resembling my prototype multiplied by ten was shaping up. Finally, on the penultimate day of construction, and to a lovely but completely hopeless manager unable to contain any longer his own design ideas for improving my tree specification, my fuse blew. He gave me his pledge that the next day all would be complete and the grim, bare grey metal of my magical tree would be sprayed and glittered to a level Walt Disney productions would be proud of.

Needless to say, hours before due delivery and my mobile `phone ringing on the hour, with anxious mall staff checking that the Winter Wonderland would arrive to their desert mall in time, I was standing deflated looking at a hopeless pile of miserable metal hoops and poles. The workshop manager, whose intentions were of the highest order but sadly unmatched by his ability, was beginning to sketch out on a scrap of crumpled paper his idea for bows that he thought would make my tree all the more splendid. I felt like jumping up and down and screaming whilst simultaneously hitting him on the head with a chunk of polystyrene, honed and carved to a torpedo mosque tower shape, that was lying in the corner of the workshop. "No, no, no," I yelled at him, feeling every strand of my fiery, Scottish, auburn hair shout in unison. "I just want you to do MY tree, to copy the prototype, as we've discussed, no bows, bells or baubles… nothing, just MY tree design… please." Sensing that 'madame' had finally lost the plot, he further crumpled his competing sketch and slipped it into his pocket, promising me that his team would work through the night to finish.

Again the deadline came and went and after a stressed and frustrated 48 hours the men eventually turned up at the mall with sections of my tree sticking out of their open truck, along with eight Indian workers and their flowing garments, clinging on for dear life and wondering what all the fuss had been about. Their jubilation at having an away day like this and in such a salubrious, air-conditioned location was spread over each individual face and all oblivious to any deadlines coming and going.

The men worked thorough the night, constructing my tree. The thing was such a monster that the chief of sewing, the same poor man who'd laboured to turn my many rolls of fabric into sails, had to perch at the top of a scaffolding tower in robes and flip flops to stitch my sails painstakingly into place, a scenario that would have had the euro-safety people running for tape to section off the condemned area.

I arrived back at the mall early in the morning to be met by the sight of the mid-section of my tree, bedecked with its fabric sails, cutting impressively through the ground floor of the mall. The tree began its sprouting from the basement floor, with its over-busy bowing alley and average coffee shop, leaving its mid-section in the ground floor and surrounded by shops selling either abayas or sunglasses, and perfume shops. Abayas, most often in black fabric and personalised with individual tailoring, fancy jewels, sequins and embroidery were the cover-up garment of choice for the ladies in the area. Ladies would cover their heads, concealing all evidence of hair, with a tightly wrapped hijab, or scarf tied around their heads and secured with a pin. Even after many years of residency in Oman, I always observed how elegantly both the men and ladies were in their traditional outfits and how gracefully one has to move when wearing such an outfit. Occasionally, ladies would appear to move so fluidly that it was hard to believe they were not being propelled on concealed wheels. The top section of my tree finally announced itself on the first floor of the mall, unexpectedly nestled alongside a branch of M&S that had newly opened in Muscat and, appropriately, the children's play area. The tree top, rushed through and untidily constructed in polystyrene, looked like an oversized marital aid and I winced at the irony of it bursting out, with not a shred of embarrassment, almost to the ceiling of this Middle Eastern mall. We'd reached 80% satisfaction if not the whole 100 and with the time constraints on our hands had done well enough to reach that.

Alongside the tree manufacture, my team and I had dressed and placed thirty regular 8 ft Christmas trees complete with lights around the mall and hung up spans of giant glittered snowflakes, some 2 ft wide, each one glittered by myself on my knees until 2 a.m. one morning.

Chapter 10
Whales and Witch Doctors

Back in Gabon, a little derailed by the inevitable happening so soon and by innocent comments here taking my mind back to my South American despair, a whale-watching trip and a cultural tour had been organised. We headed off with our picnic of freshly home-made pancakes, made in a borrowed pan and spread with a choice of rhubarb jam or chocolate spread. We also had with us enough drinking water, in the unlikely event that we were delayed. Careful explorers and modest adventurers always throw in an extra bottle of water beside a heavy sand-digging shovel. I was always accustomed to throwing in a fully-charged mobile `phone, despite the impossible network coverage which most often failed to illuminate even a single bar on the device.

After a journey of some 45 minutes on the only road here where the drive takes you long enough and on a good enough surface to manage to get comfortably through a satisfactory chunk of an iPod's playlist, we arrived at the port. On most other car trips you were lucky to reach the end of an individual song before the road under your wheels abruptly came to the end of its journey. This was the same port where we'd taken receipt of our new car only weeks earlier and where our still-to-arrive-container would finally settle its metal load down before being deposited outside our house. In Gabon, an overdue and desperately awaited container can sit infuriatingly outside your house, grass beginning to grow around the edges and bedding down, for several weeks. Strict Customs regulations here dictate that a representative from Customs must be present as the seal is broken on the metal case, as they document every item being offloaded into your home. From a comfortable seat and with a supply of fresh coffee and biscuits, the Customs' representative will peruse multiple sheets of inventory items, translated into French, and determine any excess payment due. In one particular case the officer had boarded the company `plane in Port Gentil, some 35 minutes flight away, clutching his documentation, but as the fuselage was sealed the poor man discovered an extreme fear of flying. In the end he'd had to abandon his flight, leaving signed papers and details of no excess duty charges for a relieved family. In countries such as this there can be obscure implementation of regulations. Several cars on the camp have passed their MOT by proxy, documents and inspection finalised remotely an hour's flight away.

The whale-watching boat was in much better condition than I'd expected, confirmed further by the new lifejackets stowed neatly under benches, and we exchanged polite French-style handshakes with the captain. The previous week we'd been in a small and much less organized boat, without life jackets and for a time without engine too. We'd been hippo-watching and had hired out a local boat which coughed, spluttered and croaked with animal-like sounds not unlike the hippo grunts themselves, and had given up the ghost some minutes after departure, leaving us floating in a hippo- and crocodile-strewn river. Eventually the boat handler managed to propel us back to the shore, aided by a single wooden oar. I'd spied the oar as soon as I'd taken my seat and I'd thought at the time how it would make a fabulous wall hanging, with its rough-hewn edges and functional nature. Alarmingly, we'd sat, all eight of us, in our little boat until an engine was swapped from another vessel and after much struggling our tour guides and boat handlers had the refreshed engine bolted onto our boat and we'd continued on our way to hunt down animal life. The engine this time only vaguely healthier sounding than its predecessor, at least appeared roughly able to propel us forwards.

Tsetse flies, a problem unique to Africa, are a real nuisance here and in areas of large animal density are prolific. Both the males and females are blood-suckers and the tsetse fly is partly responsible for the lack of cattle and absence of fresh milk in Gabon. We'd come prepared for our whale-watching, dressed in multiple waterproof layers and in any colour apart from blue, shades of blue, blue-black and any other colour with any intention of summoning up its blue hues. Blues attract tsetse flies and once you have drawn their attention they can bite through even the densest material, causing at best uncomfortable swellings and painful bites and at worst serious illness, such as the notorious sleeping sickness.

One member of our whale-watching party, cautioned by his wife who'd beaten him to the trip the previous week and was fully versed in the latest advice, arrived wearing a diving mask and woolly hat and cheerily greeted us whilst handing out his favoured biscuits, managing somehow to eat his own despite the silicon pressed to his face. In order to reach the sea from the lagoon where our journey began, we had to cross an area of high turbulence and he had been forewarned of a possible drenching at this point. This turbulence is the area of transition from the lagoon and the haven of the fishing fraternity out to the open sea and as such required all the skills of the boat handler to negotiate. As we set off we skirted, cheering, past several fishermen from our camp, up early to catch the tides and out doing their thing, optimistic as all fishermen are until growlingly empty cool boxes are put back into expectant car boots. From such low points, the drive home and the dissection of the individual bites that had nibbled and failed to be entirely lured would ensue. This would be followed by the many well-worn theories about why the fish weren't biting and great debates about temperature, waves and general excuses for fish disinterested in heaving their bodies up to impale themselves on jagged hooks.

Stories of successes in this pursuit quickly do their rounds in such an intimate living location. Such tales can have grown men leaping out of bed before dawn on a Saturday morning, eager to have their names added to the list of legendry fishing heroes, who've reeled in fish tipping the scales at over 50 kilos from a simple beach cast. The area of beach where these 21st century hunters do their thing is beautiful, set off with a backdrop of dense jungle. Elephants and hippo tracks are often in evidence along with, perhaps more alarmingly, crocodile tracks. These croc tracks are unmistakable with their four large footprints and long dragged tail and it shocks me to think of our men out there waist-deep in such infested water, sharks and crocs alike. For the hunter-gatherer all risks are apparently worth the fight of a multiple-kilo aquatic creature, struggling man-muscle against fin, on the end of a little line.

We adhered to all the instructions our Captain issued and grouped as many of us as possible on the back bench of the boat, holding onto our lightest and youngest child sea-tourist as per directions. Some moments later, we breathed a sigh of relief to have passed through the dangerous turbulent stretch and to safety. We continued out into a calm and beautiful sea, oblivious to the real danger imposed by such a perilous crossing, the way sightseers always are when challenging tasks like this are performed by expert hands and all looks so skilfully simple and hazard-free.

The sea was awesome, our first adventure into the seas lapping around our miles of white pristine sands here, and it didn't take many minutes for the effects of such oceanic beauty to lift my heart high. I'd scoured the sea for so many hours in Oman looking for dolphins ahead and now automatically assumed the look-out position, quickly catching sight of some tarpon skimming the surface of the water to our right. Tension and excitement were building along with multiple splashes way out on the horizon indicating the presence of our whales.

Not wishing to downplay the amazing sights of elephants walking around our camp here like some Jurassic Park film set, nor to diminish the joy of opening a curtain in the house to be met with a soft trunk pressed up against a window, tusks gently tapping the glass, whales are simply a sight out of this world. They seem to have a knowing about them and a wisdom that makes them remarkably special. On top of that, the contrast of the lightness of the sea being able to support and conceal such mammoth power takes you aback. Out of calm mirrors a whale would rise up and dive down, elegantly and with virtually no splashes, ending with a tail flourish and revealing a surprising pink-spotted underside.

I had only a few things on my mental list of sights I wanted to see in my lifetime and the flick of a tail fin of such a gentle giant was on it, etched in number two position, coming a close second to going to the northern-most point to see the spectacular and emotive Northern Lights, and ahead of the pyramids in Egypt, a place that has had an inquisitive and inexplicable pull for me since childhood. I've no huge wish-list, which occasionally perturbs me as it feels like the sort of thing one should carry around in a smart notebook of ubiquitous 'To dos'. I have reservations that such a list might unsettle life in the present moment and might make one suspend actual living, upsetting the contentment in the now. It concerns me too much that eyes might become blind to the sights of the many individual micro-scopic charms that so delight me and that joy would only be realised by placing biro ticks to a list of life's 'things to see'. So I carry no such formal list, but smiled a quiet smile in the African seas to be surrounded by tails flicking up and gracefully cutting back through water left almost undis-turbed by the graceful event. It was magical.

We spent several hours in the company of these whales, performing their elegant display. Occasionally, like in any crowd, we'd come across a bit of an extrovert, leaping out of the water and spinning its enormous hulk clear of the water and landing in a noisy belly-flop, like all the children in a public swimming pool simultaneously performing their own. I found the experience to be highly moving and, on top, we were blessed with a sea almost entirely without a ripple or swell. By now, our protective and waterproof layers had been peeled off, dive masks had been stowed away in rucksacks and we all lapped up the profusion of so many wonders strung together like this in the space of a few hours. We made for home, like a secret gang, bonded by its own unique experience, equipped with digital photos and an enthusiasm that would be lost on the landlubbers. There were no words to do justice to the sights we'd just witnessed.

As we neared the camp still reliving the wonders of the whales we'd had the joy to see, my mobile `phone regained enough signal strength to declare the arrival of a text message. "Are you interested in a Bwiti tour tomorrow?" it read. From my little knowledge of such things, I knew this was the witch doctor tours I'd heard people talk about, which were steeped in a local religious belief system. This is an aspect of Africa that intrigues many a westerner and I was no exception. "Yes, thanks. I'd love to come," I enthusiastically texted back, aware of how simple and perfectly detached a text message is as opposed to a telephone conversation. I'm often not in the mood for verbal exchanges and relieved at times to have this more distant communication at my fingertips. "Ok, great," she continued. "We'll swing by and pick you up two-ish tomorrow then." "Perfect," I concluded, excitement rising already in anticipation. Florence, a petite Scottish lady, had been living here on the camp for under a year, moving directly from Glasgow, and as such still had fresh in her mind her own lonely settling in period. She'd extended a welcoming hand when others kept theirs to their sides, showing me some of the ropes. She'd helped with the practical measures, like a lift to the supermarket, before our car had arrived and she'd lent us some towels and some beach chairs. She had two young children, both transported at the same time on her bike with the sort of ease that brings awe to folks like me who prefer the security of my own feet to wheels. A reputation as a bit of a party animal, Florence could dream up any opportunity for a knees-up, celebrating anything from the Wimbledon Final to birthdays and anniversaries of sovereigns the world over, and would always be guaranteed to out-party the rest. She provided a welcome social outlet to an otherwise socially somewhat dry camp.

My own new bike, bought amongst the many suggested items for Gabon re-location, had arrived in our mini Edinburgh shipment. Unfortunately, even before I'd had a chance to get to grips with the thing, in fact even before I sat on the saddle, a bolt broke rendering it useless until we could somehow find a replacement part from Europe carried out by a kindly soul. Such are the frustrations of this remote location. We've also had a loo seat disaster, the breaking of a fixture on one of the toilet seats brought out in this same shipment. We were thrilled beyond measure to be rid of the company seats, easily the thinnest we'd ever seen. So thin and of such poor quality that sitting at anything other than absolute perfect balance and neutral buoyancy caused the cheap design and bendable plastic to skew wildly to the side and for the user to have to counterbalance in order to avoid landing in an embarrassing heap on the floor. One evening we'd been enthralled, watching elephants in our back garden area, two large adults and two babies. To make the evening viewing clearer, we switched off all lights inside and out and called on the service of our swanky James Bond-type night vision binoculars. Certainly we had a fabulous green-tinged but very clear view in the pitch dark of the troupe of elephants, kicking and munching the ferns at the foot of a large coconut palm outside our kitchen window. Unfortunately, enthusiasm and darkness got the better of us and somewhere in the proceedings, as we'd followed them on the inside of our house whilst they walked around the exterior, my husband had gone careering into our loo, damaging our brand new seat.

I did a bit of research into the mystical Bwiti here in Gabon and unearthed a fascinating insight into the goings-on a mere few kilometres from our camp. Over recent years concerns have been growing that the country and its people are lacking a traditional religious belief and have become instead too tied to Christianity and to an extent polarized from the country's cultural roots. An increasing trend these days is a pulling back towards the Bwiti faith and a growing following of devotees to this secretive belief system.

At the core of this system is the belief that one needs to be initiated into higher realms and to be awakened. To facilitate this enlightenment, participants take part in a ceremony at which amongst the rituals is the ingestion of Iboga, 'le bois sacre', or sacred wood. Iboga is a root bark, harvested from a shrub called the Tabernanthe tree. The shrub, somewhat unremarkable in appearance, produces orange coloured fruits and can reach more than ten metres in height. The shrub, unique to this area, is renowned and revered for its ability to act as a tool for unleashing spiritual knowledge and ancestral wisdom. To prepare the root for consumption at such an initiation ceremony requires the root bark to be ground into a powder and eaten, often sweetened with honey to make it more palatable.

The Iboga contains a mysterious and most powerful psychedelic agent, granting the ability for one to see into other worlds. Bwiti shamans who eat Iboga believe they have the power to heal the sick and talk with the dead. In the western world the drug is commonly known as Ibogaine and is believed to have superpowers. Research even indicates that it may have the ability to alter the brain in such a way as to cure addictions. People who have experienced Iboga, including western students coming to such African areas to experience exotic substances, oblivious to its peculiar ability to conjure up ancestral spirits, have had more than they bargained for after ingesting the hallucinatory drug. Instead of a mild to moderate holiday 'trip' they experience a life-altering and graphic analysis of their lives, past and present. Images of people familiar to the tripper, and ghost-like representations of forefathers in feathered hats and the like, are apparently run like a movie sequence before the suspect's eyes. The ingestion of Iboga at an initiation ceremony, however, is also not without risks and can in instances lead to death. After consumption the drug must be vomited out of the system, proffering great cleansings.

The town of Gamba and its environs have expanded over the years in response to the oil industry. Its survival is largely reliant, as we are, on things being shipped and containered in here and on the mercy of large companies managing the logistics of bringing the town's shopping list in along with our own. We've a ship that sails regularly from a larger neighbouring port and brings anything, from cars to our long-awaited containers of personal items, to machine parts for the oil industry, to flour to service the local boulangerie.

Florence arrived promptly as agreed and along with three other visitors in the car, thrilled at the prospect of a glimpse into such a mysterious and intriguing religion, we headed off in the direction of the town. Not far along into our journey and just a kilometre or so past the neighbouring plantation, we were flashed by a police car, indicating that we had to stop. I'd heard of such things happening frequently here, but the importance of carrying your Carte de Séjour on your person, along with scanned copies of various documents in your glove compartment and of course the requisite currency for paying for your misdemeanours, was brought home to me.

We still had some items to add to our car safety list and police pacification bundle. We'd managed to secure our mandatory red triangle to place behind our potentially broken-down vehicle, but had yet to find a yellow safety jacket and risked having to pay a fine if this lack were discovered. Evidently the French allegiance in this country requires the implementation of European safety measures, unlike the British influence in Nigeria and the regular placing there of a small uprooted bush to demark a broken vehicle, instead of an official red triangle.

In this instance papers were perused, but we were waved on our way without any monetary exchange. Florence parked the car at the edge of the village where we were met by our tour guides, one of whom, thankfully, spoke a few words of English. The first part of our tour took us through rubbish-strewn backyards and over some upturned pirogues, or carved-out local boats which are propelled by a single oar, and down to the lagoon where some local ladies were standing knee-deep doing their laundry in the water, while children splashed around, excited by the presence of such a formidable ex-pat troupe.

I always find these occasions of us pampered folk being shown the poverty and harsh living conditions of the less fortunate, for our entertainment, to be incredibly uncomfortable. Our tour guide would be paid well and tipped for his trouble, but these poor women politely tolerated our intrusion and freely donated to us exotic digital shots that would look amazing when downloaded in our homes of abundance onto our cutting edge computers. You couldn't honestly blame them if they'd pulled faces, later requiring skilled computer manipulation to soften, or lobbed palm fruits in our direction to shoo us along.

Making ourselves as humble as we could, we assumed the tour, now passing some makeshift local food stalls, all litter-strewn and with packs of wild dogs, including several pregnant bitches, perpetuating the problem. We stopped to pay courtesy to a village elder, his face etched into lines by years of sun exposure. He was wearing a dusty cut-hat and a shirt made in the local African fabric. In this case, the printed design was of African masks and stylised palm leaves, in a monotone mustard colour, dotted with random black and white photos of the face of an African man. He was selling fish, caught in the lagoon and dried and salted to preserve them. This unappetising and fly-infested line of fish forms part of a regular consumption here, commonly eaten with some rice and some hot piri-piri sauce. I was relieved to walk away from the stench of the fish and to step out of the rubbish that was strewn everywhere. In fairness, the salted fish are mildly more appetising than the smoked catfish that are sold next to the vegetable market. They have the ability to turn my stomach inside out, lying curled up and in rows, shiny black, resembling rubber and always with a buzz of flies serenading each one.

We wandered into a few shops selling fabric and the owners apologised for the lack of selection, explaining that they were waiting for a container to arrive, soon… perhaps, or maybe later, to replenish stocks. There is no panic here and no embarrassment at empty shops and bare shelves. People are used to the way of life; things will come, shelves will be filled in the goodness of time and the lack of sales flurries have the added bonus of providing more opportunity for sipping tea and enjoying the company of neighbouring shopkeepers also finding themselves with time to kill.

Skirting the edge of the High Street and grabbing the attention of many locals amused at the sight of this expatriate caravan train being led through their little village, we took a sharp left squeezing past some wooden houses and to the area of the witch doctor's residence. We came on the temple almost immediately, with houses, temples and scrap vehicles being crammed into an area behind the shops. The temple, an open-ended wooden building with a roof of dried palm fronds, sat alone on a bed of sand with the nearest other building, home to the town's mayor, afforded the luxury of being built a mere twenty yards away. Bwiti temples are constructed to slope from the high point at the rear to the open entrance, which is so low that you have to crouch down to enter. The theory behind this inclined roof is to encourage the Bwiti spirits to linger inside. "Okay everyone, shoes off," announced Florence. Removing footwear and walking barefoot, other than in the cleansed security of my own home, is something I always find a challenge and one of the quirks I've inherited from my dad. Dad's shoes were the last thing off at night and first on in the morning. Like me, he couldn't bear the thought of being barefoot on carpets, lino, grass and the like and he'd have been breaking into a cold sweat at the prospect of having to stand on this compacted earth floor.

Swirling through my head as I bent to untie my shoes were the warnings I'd been given about making sure I didn't wear sandals when I visited the village. There is a tiny insect here with a pension for toes and for burrowing into your skin and laying eggs there, silently and secretly, only discovered much later when wriggling tracts under your skin alert you to the presence of intruders. They call them Jiggers. In a split second of rebellion, I elected to keep my white ankle socks on and followed the trail inside the temple.

The interior was dark and had a strange earthy, musty smell, with a small fire lit in the centre. A striking tall totem pole-style structure, wooden and carved with figures, reached to the ceiling and into the palm frond roof, blackened with soot from the burning fire. We were later informed that the smoke and soot from the fire protected the palm fronds from being rapidly eaten by termites, a constant problem in these parts. We were frequently having to push back termite invasions from our house and had a determined troupe trying to infiltrate by eating through the grout between our bedroom floor tiles. Occasionally we'd send them off to rethink their manoeuvres by sprinkling the area with droplets of diesel.

We were invited to take our seats on the small benches that ran along the left and right sides of the temple. At the far end of the temple and in the most prominent position there were more benches, this time with six young local boys seated and playing instruments. The boys were barechested and wearing loincloths and had distinctive white paint smeared on their faces and chests, and they wore necklaces of pectin shells for spiritual protection. The young boys appeared alarmingly spaced-out, eyes rolling in their sockets and able only to beat a drum, or rhythmically to strum bow-shaped instruments.

The most important Bwiti instrument is the M'congo. This bow-like instrument is strung with one sole string cut from the thin creepers that grow down like strands of hair from the trees. It is thought that ancestral voices are channeled through this instrument. The sound was intense and incessant, the sort of noise that if left unchecked could quite definitely cause you to lose your senses. The hypnotic pitch takes you in and becomes all-consuming as though the essence of the place mingles with the smoke from the fire seeping through your pores and infiltrating your mind. Perhaps this explained the eyes and the altered consciousness of these youngsters. I found it a shockingly disturbing and harsh spiritual environment, a sharp contrast from my aromatherapy oils, pretty tea lights and shop-bought relaxation music.

The witch doctor appeared from a door to the right of his African orchestra to conduct the presentation. A small, stout man with large brown eyes that appeared to protrude unnaturally from their sockets and which he worked well, to animate his presentation to us bemused and somewhat terrified 'blanches', or whites. He, also bare-chested and with his white body paint on, was wearing a loincloth with a small leopard skin tied around him. His protection necklace extended to his waist, large white pectin shells strung up in precise and mirrored order.

He spoke loudly and somewhat aggressively to us in French, translated by the best linguist amongst us and passed like Chinese whispers down the bench until it reached me at the end. I had it explained in my right ear that it was most important to be in bare feet and, amid a sea of feet and skin, my socks and their whiteness screamed out my dissent, cutting through even the loud, repetitive music. I sent a panic message back along the line to the linguist, who passed her reassurances back to me that "It should be okay" and that the witch doctor would let us know if there was a problem. Only mildly reassured, I withdrew my toes as far as the joints could compact and scrunched up my feet, tucking them under the bench. On occasions the main-man and his staring brown eyes made direct contact with my own blue and trembling ones and I toyed with the idea of whipping my socks off surreptitiously, to avoid the risk of him casting a spell on me. In the end, unable to bring myself to make human contact with the floor, I elected to sit tight and took the risk.

The witch doctor explained the Bwiti colours of white, black and red. The black was to represent this world, the white to represent the 'other' world and the red to symbolise blood and birth, which were painted in patterns on the wood that lined the temple. In addition he had a few props with him and one by one demonstrated their purpose or intent. He had a stick with five red tail feathers stuck in, donated (I hoped) by a willing African Grey parrot. He held up an animal horn, contorted and black and explained that this was how to call for spiritual help. "Comme une Nokia," he said cheekily, thrilled at his own humour.

He then danced his way over to the fire burning in the centre of the room, explaining that fire is also an important element for spiritual protection. He held up a chunk of Iboga and gestured to a shocked audience that we might want to eat it. With a spin he vanished back behind the scenes momentarily and returned with a blue soft-bodied wheelie case, a most un-temple-like item, and placed it on his seat. Hurriedly unzipping it, a flurry of random witch doctor items including more animal skins and horns were revealed. A length of woven raffia was fished out, neatly woven into a tight piece of fabric and with unfinished ends of raffia adding finishing tassels to the edges. In a bizarre demonstration, he then showed us the many uses for such a piece of fabric. It could be worn as a skirt, as an extra layer to his own, already two layers deep. It could be turned into a makeshift cape and we sat bemused whilst he strode up and down his temple arena modelling how that might look. Finally he positioned the material over his face, entirely, so that it reached half way down his chest. We sat, trying to remain with neutral faces and our thoughts of his madness concealed. With a sweep of his head he threw the material over his hair, so that it rose up framing his face and trailing down the back of his head. He continued the presentation looking like some raffia-bedecked Tutankhamen.

We bowed our gracious thanks to our temple chief and exited the hut, sighing a relieved sigh to be once again in freedom of the open air and to find our shoes as we'd left them, guarding the entrance. Our tour concluded outside where a healing tree was pointed out to us, rising out of the jungle that clung to the edges of this residential area. Unfortunately, we had to take his word for the healing powers as on this occasion, due to the presence of a poorly person lying under its healing canopy and in need of its power, the area was strictly no-go. With relief at leaving the omnipresent dark energy of the place, grubby white socks were placed back into boots and we headed back to our vehicle.

Chapter 11

The Contemplation of a Jogger

For several frustrating weeks we've had delivery dates of our bulging container, packed months previously in Oman, fail to result in the container actually depositing its weary load on our Monkey Road doorstep. For inexplicable reasons, our container had left from the port in Oman and landed in the Canary Islands where it had sat on the dock for five months awaiting a sailing date for Port Gentil, our nearest point of delivery. As with all these situations, clear and honest communication would have smoothed tensions but instead, week by frustrating week, the promised container had remained soaking up the heat of the sun in the Canary Islands and delaying further our sense of having fully arrived in Gabon. Unpacking such a large container and finding places for everything in a down-sized house takes weeks of work and having the job completed and the dust settled is just as important as the house being fully furnished. Packing precision and attention to detail had persuaded us to include among the necessary items large packets of grass seed, bringing to the jungle blades of grass, in a coals-to-Newcastle scenario. I'd quietly wonder at the status of the little dormant seeds and whether our personal effects would now be sheathed in a luxuriant green carpet, or whether insects may have instead munched their way through these nutritious seeds when they were done with our sacks of basmati rice.

Thanks to our small Edinburgh shipment the house on Monkey Road at least looks a little more personally styled. The company loan furniture in its dark and oppressive mahogany has been returned to the company and we we're making do with garden items instead in the living room. We have a folding picnic table, carrying two special calming candles. It is of pale wood and with a rustic charm that I'd insisted was a necessary luxury for impending beach lunches and barbeques. In an area of such unspoilt natural beauty, I'd not been able to countenance the idea of setting out marinaded meats and nibbles on a practical, plastic picnic surface. This would, I felt, have looked too incongruous in such a setting. A company wooden and raffia stool, settled in a corner beside the window, is playing temporary host to a large circular mosaic-type mirror that I'd not been able to resist the sparkle of amidst the occasional dreary shopping list items, and providing a much needed surface to deposit a coffee cup on. Adjacent to this we have a modular brown leather sofa, bought hastily at an irresistible bargain price and which allowed us to return the shockingly blue one loaned to us by the company, out of tune with our preferred palette of shades and uncomfortable to sit on. To the left of that we've positioned two further stools and topped this with a large piece of granite, bought in Aberdeen and pre-dating our children. An old church pew made of pine and with a pleasant aged patina fills a bare space of wall next to this and awaits first introduction to its identical twin in the Oman container. The idea is that the two, once united, will grace either sides of a dining table on the patio, but for now it is a welcome sight to settle eyes on in a rather minimally furnished room.

Beside the pew, and making the best of a lack of surfaces and an abundance of windowsills, my paint brushes bristle out of old coffee tins and makeshift containers. At the time, I'd thought it highly extravagant and wasteful of volume and weight to pack empty tins into an expensive freight shipment. Now, as is the case with all that we have here in this place of limited resources, life would have been a little more challenging without them. My easel too, lightweight aluminium and almost as transportable as a foldable umbrella, is wonderful. I have constantly to tweak legs and restrict canvas size in order to make it fully functional, but so far I've stood at it for many hours, pouring my heart out in paint and grateful for those slender aluminium tripod legs.

We've a little office area nestled down on a large natural coir rug. A black shiny and ultra-modern office desk and angle poise lamp indicates the 'working area' of the room, only slightly spoiled by the lack of a proper chair and other office-type surfaces and storage facilities. We've had to mismatch the ultra modern look with an uncomfortable and traditional wire-work garden chair, stuffing the back with a pillow so as to make it possible to sit in for any length of time. I've positioned strategically an elaborate brass candle-holder on the corner of it, bargained for years earlier in a souk in Oman and rediscovered neglected in a cupboard in Edinburgh. It had been dispatched to the jungle and given a new lease of life. I've tied several glistening crystals to its fancy arms that light me up each time my eyes rest on them. The light from the window behind streams in glinting shards through the swaying crystals, changing from deepest amber or coolest violet with each angled refraction.

We elected in the end only to paint two adjacent walls of the living room in our spinach colour and leave the company white on the remainder. There is a certain satisfaction to be gleaned from seeing such an enormous amount of effort and months of anticipation so graphically illustrated, and a relief that the paint pot had against many odds arrived safely from its long journey. It looks wonderful and will perfectly complement gold MDF panels I've made that are coming from Oman; but meantime, the darkness of the wall colour is a magical contrast to the sparkle from the neighbouring crystals. On the practical side, I'm still trying to persevere with the challenge of evening lighting.

And so, for the time being and until situations change and ships decide to sail to our anxiously waiting port, we'll have to maintain the improvisation. We are coping with our empty kitchen cupboards and melamine picnic ware and somehow manage to make do with our two teaspoons and few pieces of cutlery, carried in our nine cases, many months ago.

❋

I have abundant reflective time here, time for me to contemplate the idea of me heading permanently back to the UK, even before the shipment has arrived. It seems inconceivable to have such thoughts gathering momentum at a time when so much has been invested, emotionally and financially, to prepare for this jungle posting. In art materials alone, I've enough newly-bought canvas and painting materials to keep me in painting Heaven for years. Could it be possible that I'll create mayhem beyond measure by opening up my mind's thoughts for discussion and finally being ready and brave enough to take action on them?

Closing doors on one life and embarking on a new one is a highly charged and stressed affair, never mind trying to time the drama with international relocations and school benchmark exams along the way. I'd always assumed that my husband and I would go our separate ways after Oman. I thought job offers to locations in the world that are beyond my scope of coping would have cleanly and irrefutably taken an actual decision out of my hands. As if by circumstance, we'd be parted, sending designated areas of rooms and boxes of personal effects off in opposite directions. Instead, Gabon was a place that we could take Travis to, presenting no extreme security risks. Decisions were placed firmly and squarely on our own shoulders.

Amidst the all-consuming packing for Gabon, I'd managed as I'd done for years to push down the niggles in my head, rising constantly like disenchanted bubbles in a glass of soda that, try as you might to diffuse, have a necessity to rise to the surface and expel their air. I'd known in my heart of hearts years back in the location across the Atlantic, whilst sitting humiliated on a beach watching the local lovelies engage with my husband, that life thereafter was always going to be a compromise for me and I'd made certain emotional sacrifices to be able reach this stage still as a couple.

As a mother, one's protective urges are to limit damages to family situations and to an extent I'd maintained my 'trailing' role to soothe their concerns. There comes a time, however, that mums need some thunderous spark of lightning in their life. Dads too, should no longer live and cope deplete of such dynamics. We all have a right to allow clouds following our every move finally to rain down heavy and hard and to step into a brighter life, free from guilt, free from remorse and with a renewed happiness and acceptance of our individual selves. Whilst no actual statement has left my lips, I feel more and more a sense of being beyond the crossroads with the decision and to have at least made some mental pact with destiny to take whatever steps necessary to fulfil my creative purpose and to finally, fully, awaken to life.

❋

During this quiet period, my runs around the golf course seem to have much more of a mental benefit than physical. In fact, dreaded shin splints have gripped my legs leaving them feeling permanently bruised, as though someone has used the bone to sharpen the blade of a knife. They scream out at me to take some recuperative time away from the pounding. I cannot resist, however, and ignore their pleas. The emotional healing derived from every gravel-crunching footstep around this track feels intoxicatingly alluring. The idea that I've bravely faced the real and increasing threat of an elephant encounter, and taken such an out of character risk, is liberating. So out of character in fact that it somehow feels like me going into a tattoo parlour and emerging hours later with a Scottish lion rampant dancing out of my arm, glaringly red against my skin and its Celtic pallor.

Mango trees around the camp are full to bursting now with their swollen fruits and we are on heightened animal alert status. A distant trumpeting was audible on my most recent homeward run and as I passed my neighbour, ashen-faced on her bike, "There's an elephant there," she'd indicated, out of breath, gesturing to the right. Sure enough a large elephant hurried past my kitchen window as I was removing my trainers. A close call perhaps. A couple of days ago, a friend living at house 107 had her evening run aborted before reaching even the length of her car port. She'd come face to face with an elephant on the farthest side of her garden, adjacent to her washing line. Her thoughts of exercise over, she could only drink tea and watch from her kitchen window as the animal, furious now, smacked her freshly conditioned sheets on the line with its trunk before sauntering off.

Occasionally, if my confidence dips below comfortable levels, often triggered on hearing the latest wildlife encounters, I ask the guards sitting in their little security hut just prior to my right turn into my golf club exercise domains, if there are "Pas des elephants?" To date their response has been in alignment with the reassuring response that I'm after, a "Non madame," delivered with robust conviction. At this stage, mentally psyched up to expend some energy and togged up in running gear, returning home and terminating the mission is not an option. Asking such a safety question is not unlike enquiring if there are any wasps in a particular field, or perhaps worms on a football pitch. The response, whilst honest, can only barely define the truth from a specific point, limited area or moment in time. The golf course is embedded in the heart of the jungle, covering a large area, and such a safety judgment can never really be relied on. The security guards and I are aware of that fact behind our polite safety exchange and give a knowing smile to acknowledge the unspoken.

The guards have honorable intentions, however, and I'm satisfied enough that at least they haven't seen great hulking animal legs take themselves up my running route immediately ahead of me. The rest is up to the gods. If their words haven't pacified me enough, I frequently opt to run along the laterite track around the 7th green and double-back, retracing my steps along the same path, too anxious to take on the long grass and possibility of snakes lurking, especially mindful of our safety briefing weeks earlier.

I'd acknowledged the guards' bemused faces as they delivered their safety verdict. One can't help thinking that beyond their smiles they are considering the fact that if 'madame' whisked a mop or duster around her house once in a while instead of hiring local help to do it, or took over the gardener's job raking leaves and building unnecessary little bamboo fences, she would be spared the stress of having to burn calories in this enforced and solitary way.

I think about how much Travis would protest at the prospect of this going over old ground and retracing steps along a path. He particularly digs in his stubborn paws when I attempt to take him on a walk that doesn't flow in full circle but that takes him past bushes and lamp posts already weed on or sniffed at, or both. I have to complete the walk with an eight kilo lump of unco-operating fluff and determined spirit, refusing to engage his legs and with his collar, slightly over-sized, making its way over his head enough to become snagged against one of his ears. His face at times like this rises to the full Jack Russell expressiveness and even without words he fully conveys his deep resentment of the proceedings.

I consider too how wrong we are for assuming that a return journey can never retrace one's footsteps, foolishly thinking that we have the power to 'know' a certain path by heart. For all we do know a turn-around and retracing of steps can yield up wholly different obstacles, challenges and even pleasures, to the outward journey. The wind might change from a head to a tail, or vice-versa. One might encounter someone who would have remained behind in one's footsteps and unnoticed. In the case of

Gabon, an elephant, intrigued by the sight and sound of something much smaller making an inordinately loud puffing noise may have decided to follow the tread-marks running shoes have imprinted in the gravel. It makes me consider that nothing in life can ever really totally be retraced. Moments change perception and the universe has a way of throwing something unexpected in your path. It's wiser to assume a retrace as based on some vague familiarity, but one must be prepared to notice and react to the differences that may spring up along the way. A simple little gravel path, orange-tinged and deliciously crunchy underfoot, like the sound of a home-baked ginger biscuit being eaten, can teach us about life, if we block out mental chatter and let thoughts float to the surface.

Unlike the 24-hour staff cover in Nigeria as a result of the staff living on the premises in the BQs, the domestic help situation in Gabon is refreshingly a more distant affair. They arrive here daily from the village, either bussed in by the company or by tired, rusted blue and white taxi.

On our first morning on the camp, I'd opened the kitchen door to the garden to be shocked by the sight of a man standing in the doorway of the little garden shed we'd inherited, wiping dripping bright yellow gloss paint from his hands and brush. We'd exchanged pleasantries and he explained in French that he was the former gardener of house 120 and was looking to have his employment continued, seamlessly, by us. I felt mildly irritated by his decision to hang onto our shed key and made a mental note that this sent out advanced warning signs into possible negative character traits. I'd have preferred things if he'd knocked on the door and surrendered the key instead, and that his re-employment status would have looked less bleak than it now was.

This was my first real sense of language frustration and a rude awakening for my fatigued Higher Grade A pass, gleaned decades ago. In the end, amidst much gesticulation, curtailed only by the excited Jack Russell struggling on my hip and injecting me repeatedly with painful claw scratches, I managed to convey my desire to be the key-holder to the little wooden shed and its pot of bright paint. I told him to come back later, "Plus tard", and to give me some time to make my mind up. He bade me a polite farewell along with promises, shouted from the foot of the driveway, to build a little house for the dog, elevating his future employability only marginally.

Each morning for the next several days and always at a precise 7 a.m. I'd answer the door to his regular appeals for my decision. Slowly, also, a steady stream of ménagères began to knock on my door, prospecting for house cleaning work. In some cases the interview was conducted and their eligibility dismissed within minutes of their optimistic knocking on the door. Travis would rush out, bristling with his usual exuberance to greet the visitors and would filter out those who, too afraid of his presence, took to their heels. The interview would be concluded and the position would remain vacant without a word having been exchanged. In the end, relying on the gut instincts that pointed to the most suitable employee, and wishing to end this daily circus of knocks, bright floral local prints and strained French conversations, I selected a quiet and unassuming lady, still petrified of dogs, to work for us.

Over the weeks, she has scrubbed and scraped all surfaces inside and outside the house, removing the nests that weekly surreptitiously try to sneak into location. Travis has never given up his desire to befriend this new regular face and she in response has not let up her shrieks of resistance if he strays too near to her territory at the sink. On occasions this impasse stresses me, exacerbated by the barks and the French language cries, and I walk to another room until the brouhaha has settled. I try to be patient. Rome wasn't built in a day, after all.

We've also employed a gardener, Stanley, who mercifully speaks English and who has become the key-holder of the shed, by decision as opposed to by default. We leave him quietly to do his thing in the garden and he is slowly managing to confirm to the outside world that new tenants are in occupancy, busying himself with the construction and installation of a little bamboo fence. Neither my husband nor I are particularly hung up on the little fence, covering metre by growing metre, but we leave his creativity to flourish unchecked. Bamboo fences seem to be his thing, his trademark, and just as I need to be left to paint flowers and leaves and become irritated when I'm asked "Do you do portraits?", a fence-builder must be left freely to create and delineate boundaries he sees as important. Hours of labour have gone into sawing down lengths of giant, thick bamboo from a neighbouring plant and then reducing the magnificent lengths to workable sections for the fence that stands at some 30 cm high, reduced more than tenfold from its former spectacular towering beauty. The once roundly healthy bamboo plant has an ever-increasing gaping hole in it and I quietly walk past on my dog walks, embarrassed at the realization of what we have done. By allowing our gardener free reign we'd been complicit in robbing this beautiful plant specimen that was growing for all to admire and I shudder at the lush canopy of bright leaves that now look so sparse.

Stanley's gardening efforts and boundary markings are perilously close to being damaged, trampled under elephant foot, each time trunks strain against the adjacent mango trees to pluck off the ripened fruit, leaving deep gorges in the tree bark. Giant footprints and mango branches litter the ground each morning, along with a scattering of sucked mango stones, eliminated from elephants' mouths, satisfied that they have extracted sufficient nutrition. Depressions are left in the soil and clearly defined toe detail that prompt Travis's hair to adopt an involuntary Mohican style, on inspection. One wonders what must go through his head, investigating footprints that are big enough for him to curl his entire little body up in.

Stanley is an amiable enough man and seems to serve his time in and around the garden environs, albeit making slow progress, but there are days when I opt to keep conversations to a brief "Good morning, Stanley. It's looking good," and "Goodbye, Stanley." Though polite and hard-working, his meekness and subservience have begun to irritate me. The other day the doorbell rang and I'd answered it to find Stanley cowering beside the door, holding an outstretched hand which contained five little mangos. "Can I take de mangos?" he'd whispered, barely making eye contact with me. "Ees it ok?"

"Of course you can take them," I replied, handing him a little black plastic baguette bag which, hopeless for baguettes, I thought would come into its own as a mango transporter. "I don't use them, Stanley," I replied, finishing, "It's really pas de probleme, go ahead," despite his English. A "pas de probleme" brings a universal smile here and feels sufficiently on the top of one's tongue to use liberally in conversations, unlike French phrases of more construction and grammar that lurk in dark, reclusive corners just when you need them most.

I went back inside as Stanley headed off past the window with his little black bag and I couldn't help wincing at his intense timidity. After all, on a nightly basis the elephants ram and raid our trees, chomping whole branch sections off and leaving mango stones they've sucked dry and whole mangos they have not been tempted by to rot. A gardener picking up five mangos for his personal consumption from beneath a few trees that happen to be outside a property that we happen to be in, is neither here nor there. I then question my apparent heartlessness; after all, surely Stanley's trustworthiness should be honoured and not chastised? I postulated that his over-politeness and under-assertiveness I occasionally see in myself. Multiplied ten-fold in our gentle gardener, it made me recoil.

Ahead of our English-speaking gardener, we'd had on trial a lovely local Gabonese man with the brightest smile and jauntiest of hats, but the poor man was only able to communicate with us in French. Unfortunately, combined Higher Grade French qualifications of my husband and I didn't manage to convey a single word of instruction to this lovely man. The last straw was seeing my husband struggle on our doorstep with his laptop in his hand, reading out a translation from an Internet search for the French words to convey our wish to have a tree removed. The poor man unable to comprehend, and my husband pointing to the little sentence on his screen, reliably translated, was like some comedy farce. I still have pangs of guilt each time I walk past him, in his little hat, raking his leaves in some of the other gardens, that we'd failed him with our inadequate language skills.

I get a lot of inspiration for my creativity when I'm alone in nature, repeatedly pounding one foot after the other on the golf course and I consider and question what it is that I see my life purpose to be. I think about contingencies and how I build in no contingency into my huffing and puffing round the golf course, should a wildlife encounter necessitate me getting out of there fast. I think too about my interior work and reflect that my design contingency was always to put my hand into my own pocket. No 10% was ever sneaked into material costs to be passed onto unsuspecting clients. If a scheme needed a special something that budget didn't permit, I'd dip into my own reserves in order to make sure that nothing would stand in the way of me being satisfied that I'd delivered my grandest design.

I think about my entrepreneurial enterprises and how this element of self-funding has come into play with much that I've embarked on. Be it under-charging for a painting or overly discounting home interior items bought in Africa and sold in the house in the Middle East, I always pay closest attention to making sure the recipient is fully happy and less to the business strategy. I reflect too that, unless one is very highly regarded and in the top percentage of artists, it is well nigh impossible to make a living from selling paintings. As I cross round by the impressive large bamboo that occupies the centre of the 9ᵗʰ fairway and which creaks hauntingly with its large stems swaying, I reflect that my intensity and urge for painting is more seated in a desperation to 'say something', to convey a message through use of colour, shape and energy and by surrendering the essence of my heart to each canvas. I have an urgency to send messages of hope and of inspiration resounding out from my art. The pleasure and relief of that is more than enough compensation for me.

As I head for the homeward drag, I reason that my art is about stirring people to stir something in themselves. I skirt past some potholes in the road, as I've been doing for weeks, and clearly defined to my right is a pothole shaped exactly like the continent of Africa on a map. I'm stunned by how perfectly the laterite depression, orange and carved out by rain, had created a crater that mirrors the landmass of the entire continent. I couldn't believe I'd run past here so many times before oblivious to this miracle.

Amazingly, as if through some symbolic significance, just before leaving the house for my run I'd unearthed in the washing machine door, as I pulled out wet towels, a section of rawhide dog chew that Travis must have been working on for some time. I'd held it up, soggy from the wash and sweet from the fabric conditioner, and noticed without any doubt that, with its neatly nibbled edges, the chew also resembled the continent of Africa. So delighted was I with the discovery that I declared it out loud to an empty house and went over specifically to point out this wonderment to the dog, who gave it a sniff and rejected it and its newly perfumed smell from any further chewing.

※

I'd be honoured to think that any of my pieces of art, or a sentence of my written words, might have the ability to inspire. To slow down the chattering of a mind's workings, to allow inspiration to float to the surface. Perhaps enough stillness may be generated to ignite a creativity spark in someone, so they can spot their own cratered continents and poignantly shaped nibbled dog chews concealed around them.

There are days when even running around a verdant golf course, carefully avoiding stepping on a single blade of grass, aren't enough to suppress certain internal anxiety levels. Not even the knowledge that my angels are alongside me and guarding over my safety is able to detune my mind from animal precautions being on heighten alert. These prickly days are becoming more frequent just now with the rainy season marking its presence, and often back-to-back 24-hour unrelenting downpours. Water tables have risen to the extent that the laterite paths in the golf course vicinity, normally several clear feet of dry land above water, now have lagoon edges licking at their sides.

The area of jungle path that one has to pass through before arriving at the golf course has a new tension to it. The creaks and cracks emitting from the trees and occasional thuds of monkeys falling entirely to the ground, shocked and with ripped branches in their hands, encourage my already quickened pulse to step into overdrive. Many animals will have been displaced from their homes due to the rising water levels and I can't help focusing concerns on the proximity of their rainy season hide-outs. Residents located in houses that flank this rising water tell tales of being able to cast a fishing line from their patios and reel in a fish only some 15 feet from their living rooms.

I have therefore built a new safety measure into my running, in addition to electing now to carry my bulky mobile `phone in a bum bag during my jogs, its acidic pink colour completely blowing any co-ordination there might have been to my running gear. I often wish I'd acquired a taste for the compact and wafer thin microscopic mobile `phones, so tiny they can be stored in the minutest pocket. I have an inclination to `phones with qwerty keyboards and five hundred functions of which I only use three and which are always encased in oversized non-jogging bodywork. I now stop for a few minutes at either side of this jungle stretch and take some deep breaths before running with my full pelt until I'm safely beyond the woods, either on the orange golf path or on the safety of the grey tarmac of the camp. I can tolerate for these few minutes top speed fleeing, skipping over cratered African continents and running the gauntlet of dead frogs prostrated on the surface. I'm perplexed these days to find the roads round the camp littered with deceased insect and animal bodies. Along with the frequent orange puddles full of dissolved laterite, the place has a semblance of a giant bowl of bouillabaisse soup with crusty and squishy lumps of flesh suspended in this watery base.

Mangos on the camp are ripening before our eyes and elephants unable to wait for the safety of dusk now arrive, sometimes as entire little families, to dine in the prettiness of our succulent camp. Frighteningly often, I'd come back from my run to be met with a barrage of calls from neighbours warning that there was elephant life dangerously near to our house. One evening I'd been on the `phone to the UK and heard a loud trumpeting in close proximity to the house. Aware of the open French doors and an unusually high pitch to Travis's barks, sensing something fearful on the horizon, I'd promptly dropped the earpiece still connected to its international call and expensive long-distance tariffs, and ran to bring him into safety. To the left of the patio was a beast of an elephant and I couldn't help thinking that the little trumpet noise seemed ill-matched to such a generous animal. He appeared angry, kicking stumps of trees and pushing his head full force into the trunk of a tree to try and dislodge some ripened mangos. He was creating a flurry of attention, cars had parked beside the house, drivers jumping out with camera `phones at the ready; probably, I'd assumed they were people on business trips, not familiar with the danger these animals pose. Curiosity now getting the better of me, the animal walking out of sight and lighting conditions conducive to my first daylight elephant snap, I grabbed a camera and jumped into the car, heading off on the hunt for a good shot.

It was obvious that this animal had created a stir and possible to track its passing presence by the number of residents out of their houses, eyes trained in a certain direction. I followed their stares and moments later seemed to hit on the eye of the storm, three security guards fleeing left, right and centre and the occupants of the vehicles parked at my house standing in the safety of a large tree trunk, amused at the events unfolding. I tentatively steered my car past them and caught sight of the massive beast angrily flapping its ears and chasing a fellow newcomer into his house. It was evident he was prepared to take greater risks for his wildlife shot than I was and evident from the grin on his face that he was thrilled by the excitement of having a rampaging elephant on his tail. I thought better of making any closer advances, wishing my car was a more empathetic dark green instead of glaring white, and returned home postponing the photograph to a future date.

Later that evening my next door neighbour called to alert me to a family of elephants in touching distance of my patio and its mosquito screen. "You've elephants, adults and babies, right in front of your window," he said, as I tried, momentarily, to place his Dutch tones.

"Oh really," I responded, peering out into the dark.

"They are looking right at you," he continued. Straining my eyes, I managed to pick out the silhouettes, a mum and dad and two babies reaching trunks high into my trees and plucking mangos off.

"Oh yeah, I see them. Thanks," I offered up and focused my attention through the glass. In a split second it crossed my mind how guilty I'd felt for having been so immersed in my laptop and oblivious to such external, natural activities. I was also disappointed that I'd been sighted, hair tied up in a matronly scrunch and the dreaded reading glasses perched clinging to the tip of my nose, declaring me to be 40+ in the way these things do. Still, I was appreciative of his thoughtfulness and made a mental note to be more on the alert in future and to be able occasionally to offer my own neighbourly animal up-dates instead of becoming indebted in this way.

Chapter 12
The Ship Docks

There's something about the stir of this animal life that prompts a deeper inspection of life and a questioning of one's direction. As jungle days clock by and shipments are no closer to being delivered the urge for me to somehow break free from the emotional shackles in my life intensifies. I feel as if I've walked a certain path in life up to this moment, which has run its course. When I examine my relationships and my broken family in Scotland, I ponder any part my own overly sensitive nature has had in distancing myself from those I love. I've tried to make light of the situation to friends, to bring some dry humour to the notion that I have more people on my non-communication list than on the communication one. It's easy to laugh outwardly at such analogies of estrangements, but the reality of living with relationships running like dry sand through fingers is sometimes a cross that is hard to bear.

My dad is excused, since his disappearance from being three-dimensionally large in my life was not his own choice. In fact there are times that my dad feels closest of all, behind my shoulder, encouraging my progress. My heart is heavily laden with the fractures to the family, my mum, sister and twin still not united after more than a decade. I made tentative attempts several years ago to try to mend the broken bridges and to bring the family back to sweetness, instead of these sour disjointed particles. My efforts, whilst well intended, seem further to split and damage any chunks of unity remaining, like an axe-man, not content with splitting his logs, who opts to continue hacking, separating the wooden pieces over and over until matchsticks are all that remain from a once solid piece of wood.

My mediation attempts have brought an unhealed wedge between my sister, my mum and myself. I sit in the quietness of my home in the jungle and have plenty of time to consider the causes and effects that have brought about such estrangements and to consider if any positives can have been gleaned from such pervading negativity. Some days, it seems that the ease of 21st century communication has coincided so ironically with those I love stepping back from me, making the pain all the more palpable and the absence of communication all the more obvious.

In this heightened period of reflection, I think about estranged sisters, entire families of in-laws and old friends and wonder what significance all the contacts that've fleeted into my life have had. I know that some of this disharmony must be a part of a plan to pull out characteristics of myself that have a need to rise majestically to the surface out of their darkened corners. Above all, I have to keep on loving, this most elusive of all, the unconditional stuff and not to harbour bitterness and anger. I have to accept the ebb and flow of relationships and that some were meant to float off detached like the seeds from a dandelion clock that break free and re-seed in new soil. Sooner or later, all relationships end in separation as we know it and this makes unconditional love all the more essential. This can be the only way to approach a union, to love wholeheartedly and unreservedly for the joy that gives and what is returned is a bonus. Love must be freely given and to hold a hand out expectantly for some form of acknowledgement or payment negates the essence of it.

Family estrangements are among the hardest to deal with. I think of happier childhood days and of a busy and nurturing home environment. I wonder if the signs of the fractions to come were evident then and that childlike naivety failed to spot them. I conclude that we had a loving childhood, surrounded by the sort of warmth that generally fills a happy home. There were never any grand dramas, or ever the sense that our little pack was festering beneath the smiling facade, other than at times an overly polite atmosphere. Perhaps the odd grievances that might have been better set free into the air were prevented from airing and instead of issues being discussed, and perhaps resolved, they were swallowed painfully down and ended up settling as bumps and stickiness under the skin. These suppressions have a tendency to become a part of who you are and provide a wonderfully fertile ground for negative self esteem thoughts to flourish.

I try to take a day at a time and keep my mind off notions that the family, as it was, will never be again. It hardly seems credible that my sister and mum will never reunite and occasionally have an overwhelming feeling of futility descend around me. I've always been drawn to the films and the story books that have resolved happy endings and I struggle to make sense of the relationships spiralling off around me. The only thing that seems to make sense to me is that every minute detail and every part of those scenarios is meant to be and that instead of trying to shape and control outcomes and grasp onto with all your might hands slipping from your reach, it is truly about fully letting go. Relationships, like butterflies, are best left to fly free and one must remain a place that the butterfly when set free will of its own volition want to return to, a place of peace and love and of non-judgement instead of any thoughts of chaining, shackling and duty.

I reflect on myself as a child and how self-contained and content I was growing up in the security and protection of the family unit, at my most blissful when all around me were healthy and harmonious. My first brushes with sadness were the occasional demise of my many pet hamsters, tenderly looked after and luxuriously housed, but which inevitably and all too soon succumbed to their short life-span allocation. I remember one occasion when I'd opened my hamster's cage to be met with a frozen body in mid-stride. The cage was an elaborate warren of coloured Perspex tubes and Snowball, an albino long-haired animal, had obviously been struck down just as he had entered the first tunnel of his cage. It was necessary to pass through this en-route to his dining quarters despite this quadrupling a possible journey time of a more direct tunnel route. His body was alarmingly now in suspended action and unable to bring myself to face the truth I let out a distressed scream that sent all members of the house running to my aid, in a manner not dissimilar to the scenes I'd witnessed in TV hospital dramas. As I concealed part of my view behind my fingers, as one does when watching a horror scene unfolding, my dad fished the stiffened creature from his tunnel, disappeared to the living room with him and began to follow instructions, shouted by me through the astragal glazed door that separated me from the intensity of the drama. I felt it easier to deal with the trauma from this distance, despite the fact that my hamster's fancy cage sitting beside me and a conspicuously open door bore all the evidence of the severity of the goings-on.

Even in those days, without the luxury of the wealth of Internet knowledge available at touches of buttons, I'd somehow come across tips for hamster revival and cautions about apparent death often being confused as an innocent hibernation. My first instructions were to wrap the tiny body in a towel and to massage it, in the hope that whiskers could be encouraged back into twitching life. The family obligingly carried out my request and, moments later when the little body retained its rigidity, appealed for the next step in bestowing of life. Following my pleas, a hairdryer was plugged in and could be heard training its warm breeze onto the white fur. But in vain. The animal was no closer to being able to resume its journey along the fancy tunnel-work in the cage. Next step was to blow some life-giving air down its throat, which I thought would surely have the poor beast awakening from its icy slumber. I opened the glazed living room door just enough to throw in a blue and white striped surgical tool, a plastic straw, to assist the operation and awaited the shouts of success. Sadly that had also failed to do the trick and with only one remaining procedure up my sleeve, my tears of despair had begun to stream from my eyes. As evidence of the supporting family I was a part of, my dad now followed my unrelenting instructions and began to drip some drops of his finest brandy into Snowball's mouth, watched by my mum and concerned sisters. Eventually, after some time and to spare all of us, not least the little lump of solid fur, further stress the animal was pronounced dead. My tears turned to rivers as a little box, hastily emptied of its pristine unstruck golf balls, was padded with soft, pink toilet roll and Snowball was tucked in. He was later laid to rest under the red rose in the garden and his presence indicated by a cross of twigs I made in his honour.

In Gabon, even before I'd opened my eyes that morning, I'd had a sense of something big hanging in the air and on rising could feel a certain excitement, not unlike the sort that is felt awakening on a crisp, Christmas morning. I continued about my normal routine, liberally applying mosquito repellent and bending to attach Travis's lead to his collar. I sometimes wish Travis was able to stroll at one with me, unleashed and free, but electing to walk at a regular distance to my stride merely because he wants to and not because he has to. Somehow, the pleasure of walking him is diminished by this ubiquitous lead chaining him to me and which I have to tug on repeatedly to encourage him to make any forward progress at all. Jack Russells love nothing better than to stand rooted to the spot sniffing and decoding any scents hidden in the grass and surrounding soil, moving forward only at the sight of a bird that has tantalisingly flown low enough for him to catch, or at a whiff of an even better odour wafting from another direction requiring the attention of his long snout.

They say that if you want to make a dog become attached to you then it is first necessary for you to stop chaining them to you in this manner. Those with expertise will also say that a loved and loving Jack Russell should at all times be tethered and that many owners have learned to their cost that the Jack Russell bent for hunting and for trailing a scent overrides any human bond. A Jack Russell in such pursuit will push to the back of his head any thoughts of snugly beds and favoured fluffy toys and even of jars of doggy treats, openly and enticingly placed in his view, and opt to run to his freedom never to be seen again.

Travis and I progressed around the camp and, as I regularly have to do on each occasion, I tugged him protesting past the piled up leaves and rotting mangos at the end of each driveway. Several if not all of my chiropractor sessions in Muscat were to repair damage to the lower back that this battle of wills between myself and such a powerfully stubborn animal had caused. I worry at the high risk of his foraging in these leaf piles, knowing how enticing they are also to snakes. At times, when his spirit and determination reigns supreme over mine, I give up momentarily and tell him to go ahead at his own peril, knowing that I'm so exhausted by the twenty or more rotting piles of curled up leaves and alcoholic-like stench of old mangos already negotiated that I've no reserves left for these mental games.

We met a fellow dog walker and chatted for a while, whilst the dogs, delighted at the unexpected opportunity, sniffed, licked and growled at each other simultaneously. Sally and I had known each other on the previous Oman posting. She was a friend of a friend and though we'd not socialised with any frequency in Gabon, we both had a mutual appreciation for our great friend, Margaret.

Margaret had been a larger than life wonderful character, with the sort of laugh that would make its infectious presence known no matter how much ambient noise there was. She had unique vibrancy to her and a confidence in her own skin that allowed her to remain completely true to herself whilst the rest of us were grappling to find ourselves, in the latest fashion, or plunging headlong into the current other 'in' thing to be into. Margaret was never influenced by something as superficial as the 'new black', or the trendy way to think for the season. She'd also had a pet parrot, an African Grey, caged in a large aviary on her patio. I still have a tiny scar on a finger from the bird's decision to stop in its tracks my attempts to stroke his head. I think of my friend every day, when the flocks of African Greys squawk past overhead here in this natural wonderland and think how much she would love to see them wild like this.

I wonder a lot about the role the fashion industry plays in the distortion of one's trueness and how much a desire to go with the pack strips one of the confidence to stand one's own ground and to rise up beyond people's shallow judgements, based on the latest look. As a fashion lover myself, I can reflect on periods of my life where my outward clothing statements were something I'd given too much consideration to. It's possible that in Nigeria, as I'd tried to deal with the gut-wrenching feeling of walking past the boys' empty bedrooms a multitude of times in the day, I'd become overly focused on denim styles and having the latest heel in my wardrobe to fill emotional voids.

I remember feeling totally out of touch on home leave occasions to the UK that came two or three times a year. In Nigeria, I didn't shop, drive myself, go to the bank or receive or send mail directly. We didn't even have access to the Internet at home. My husband was the frontline for the lion's share of the chores, the mail arriving addressed care of his indicator code and the bank being situated in his office complex. Much was removed from spouse action and whilst this made life easier, such as avoiding lengthy bank queues, you soon begun to feel less of the independent person you felt you'd been when you arrived. I'd also struggled at times with the camp extroverts and occasionally felt overtly self-conscious in what was, at times, like living in a goldfish bowl. To an extent we lived our life on a daily stage and acted our roles every day. Despite the camaraderie on the Nigerian camp, you knew you were performing to a packed theatre of critics, pens at the ready to detail every slip and slide.

I recognised in myself a pulling towards the feel-good factor of having the latest fashion dictate in your possession and to an extent allowing pieces of cloth and bias-cutting skills to speak for me. Perhaps my way of compensating for the inability to climb on a table with my dancing shoes, like so many did and with such aplomb, was to luxuriate in the comfort of knowing that at least I was well turned-out in the shadows.

I sometimes think back to my youth, to times that I'd dressed myself in a manner that would be classified as contra-fashion. In my early days of motherhood, I was so blissfully content and complete in my role in life that I didn't even own a pair of denims, never mind having to have the latest fashionable version of them. I always found them too cold to put on in a cool climate and preferred the warmth of woollen varieties of trousers or cords.

I think in recent years and with the media and advertising influence, slavish following of fashion has reached dangerous levels. The notion that material acquisitions are a panacea to happiness is setting up many of the religious devotees for a full personal crash in years to come. Shopping pursuits can be dangerously alluring and it's easy to succumb to a fashion fix to get you over a tough bump or out of a little dip. Of course, the momentary high of having been treated as a valued someone by eager assistants, counting up their commission on fingers behind their backs, fades even faster than the indigo dyed fabric. I recognised in myself the healthiness of the young mum who had so much happiness within she really didn't consider any statements that her clothing might be making, to the contrast of the individual in Nigeria who, lacking in personal confidence levels, turned even if only slightly to external salvation.

❈

In the early days of my husband's postings, when life took us for a period far from tropical climes to the cool north of Scotland, I'd befriended a lovely Mother Nature girl, Alice. She oozed style, yet in such a personal and uncontrived way. Her passion was for life beyond the material and her house constantly ran with a plethora of tiny four-legged creatures. When visitors called, cats would run the wall of death over sofas and swipe alarmingly at unsuspecting ankles, selecting the dog-lovers for particular provocation. Alice had rescued a little stray dog, doubly incontinent, but admittedly with the cutest face. A relaxing chat over coffee was fraught with this ticking time-bomb of elimination peril.

I'd leave her house, relieved to be in the fresh air, brushing an ensemble of cat and dog hairs from my clothes, but reflecting that there was something this girl was getting right in life that we were all struggling to find in our own. It wasn't that her house was an interior disaster. Her place was well styled and co-ordinated, in fact she had an eye for it; but that wasn't all of what she was about. No textured cushion or patterned rug would entirely win her heart. It was most definitely a case of her owning the items, and certainly not the other way round.

I met up with her years later and she had remained as real and unchanged by life's passing as she ever had been and at times stuck out awkwardly from the plastic pack of us huddling to collect our children from school. You wondered if she ever cast a glance at the arms draped with the latest must–have bags and the designer sunglasses perched on the top of high-maintenance hair around her, but most probably she wasn't even inclined to notice.

❋

The country across the Atlantic had been so overtly based on outward appearances that I wonder if souls and true essences of people are ever unveiled there. It still disturbs me to think that a displayed silicon chest and tease of a toned thigh are the yardsticks to measure a person's worth by. An observer awarding a highest scoring '10' to such a lady, reveals a lack of comprehension into the deeper and lasting human elements that shine on for eternity, long after silicon chests have had their packaging removed and plump skin has wizened. It's no coincidence that many of these ex-pat-local married liaisons have little longevity in them and many of these ladies addicted to external validation of their worth cannot resist the urge to lure others with their charms and swiftly move on to new male challenges. Separated husbands are left perplexed by true love ending as spectacularly and abruptly as it had arrived.

Thanks to my respect for Margaret, I'd faced one of my lifelong fears of having water over my face and learned to scuba dive under her guidance. She was entirely at home under the ocean and, removed from this, her spirit sank. She regularly organised dives for us housewives and she'd capably coordinate us all and oversee our equipment. We'd often be buddied up together and even a bulky demand valve lodged in her mouth and the lack of actual voice didn't deter her from her eager communication. We'd chat and enthuse about the delights swimming past our eyes or hidden in rocks and plan our evening's socialising.

Though only in occasional contact these days, I often think of her and of the fact that she was so remarkably intact as an individual and so immune to concerns of people's opinions of her. I balance this with the knowledge that so many of us since those Oman days of naivety have had to learn much about ourselves that she has always known. She was always a wise soul and a positive character and never looked at any challenges encountered with anything less than an excited determination to make the best of the situation. Sally and I exchanged any snippets of information we knew of Margaret's whereabouts and agreed that we thought she was still living in the Far East and had been able to continue her life's diving passion in the location.

I came back from the dog walking and took some time, in the privacy of the bedroom and away from the house-help's vigorous sweeping, to meditate in the calm space giving me a chance to energise for the day ahead. Next step, and following my automatic routine, I made a cup of tea before checking my mail. And there it was, in my inbox, sitting in unopened bold type: 'Sea Freight Delivery'. My head was abuzz of all emotions simultaneously, as well as hastily worked out calculations determining precisely when our rusty 40 ft container, finally closed shut at 2 a.m. in Oman, would be deposited outside our house on Monkey Road.

For so many days, weeks and months I'd familiarized myself with intricate details of the camp and street environs. There's a particularly sculptural tree which embraces the crossroads adjacent to our own Monkey Road. Its gnarled and etched trunk splits into clearly defined and balanced feminine arms, reaching gracefully up and out, gesturing warmly to anyone who cares to notice amidst its soldierly and more regularly upright neighbours. Between the arms, at the top of the thick trunk, a cluster of wood and bark has formed itself into an inclined head that seems to offer up a loving nod of acknowledgement, without a sound or a movement, apart from the occasional gentle tremble of leaves above.

On my many hours of dog walks, I've paid attention to the type of gardening statements residents in our Gabon camp have made to indicate their occupancy and noticed that leaf by leaf, despite elephant challenges and dismay at being apart from our things for so long, our own garden has surprisingly reshaped and reseeded itself into a pattern more of our own hand. I've smiled at the ornamental animals made by a local craftsmen that crouch and peer from bushes and around corners of other homes - diminutive hippos, elephants, leopards and the like, all brightly painted and all indicating a level of settlement and contentment of the residents in occupation. I've sometimes promised myself that when we were similarly settled, I'd order up a Jack Russell, leg cocked against a tree, and amused myself with the irony of this spectacle as I continue on my way with the live version.

There's usually a container or two in residence here, incongruous, modern and metal and of the other world. They are particularly out of kilter with our natural jungle environs. They signify the arrival of a family's belongings and mark the final hurdle in settling in, as though for all the stress of preparation, shopping, strangeness and awkwardness endured, you have been awarded a 'pass' and the ceremonial reuniting with your estranged goodies is your reward. They also represent the end, the packing up and moving on, the saying "Goodbye" to friends made and to such rare and magnificent unspoilt places as endless jungles in Gabon. With the packing over and the boxes banished an eerie calm descends, like the lull before the storm until the reality of the cycle of visas, shopping and strangeness resumes, as predictably as autumn follows summer.

On sighting a freight container, I always take a few minutes to consider that no matter the colour, the rusting condition or the cubic metre capacity nor even the contents, these metal boxes are full of emotions, from turmoil to sadness and from excitement to fear. It matters little really what the material content is, modern and funky or traditional and well-worn, whether the boxes are full of brightly coloured children's toys or hobby materials and books to fill the gap of empty nests. The enormity of the relocation process and the emotional human toll transcends material possessions and cannot be underestimated. Now, finally our time had come and perhaps contentment would descend on our house and especially me.

Chapter 13

Opening the Freight

I thought back to the nine months previously, as our container was finally sealed shut in our driveway in Oman. For five unrelenting hours and the culmination of three days of packing, our able team of six hard-working Indian packers had turned, twisted and coaxed every one of our three hundred boxes and miscellaneous odd–shaped items, mummified in cardboard swathes. It was like some Krypton Factor puzzle trying to maximise every cubic centimetre of space. As if the unbearable 45 °C heat and energy-zapping humidity weren't enough, the poor men were equipped with no lights. Eventually, we focused our car headlights in their direction and left the engine running for the equivalent of a non-environmental drive from Oman to Dubai, only in this case without the border checks or the buzz of the metropolis and its tedious traffic congestion. I'd wished we'd thought of the solution earlier but energy levels all round were drained and thoughts and solutions processed slowly whilst the poor men had struggled in the dark. Before the door was sealed shut, I'd managed to find a chink of energy from my fatigued system and scraping up a bundle of oddly twisted branches I handed them to the man on the door of the container. "Could you manage to find a small space for these?" I appealed to him, almost appalled at myself for not being content with a container that was already so evidently packed to capacity.

"No problem, Madam," came the familiar, polite and accommodating reply. "Thanks so much," I finished, as I handed over the bundle.

It seemed vulgar. Not content with the excess and indulgence the container already represented, including new washing machine, dishwasher, TV the size of a small cinema screen and a plethora of wholesale stock for our remote Gabon location, here I was stealing from the land. I turned my shame-face away as quickly as I politely could. It was too complex to explain that the sticks had been gathered by the boys when we did a family 'Wadi' walk in Oman and held some sentimental significance. This trek, awesome in its beauty and breathtaking in its views, was one of the fondest memories of our posting to Oman. The walk is probably one of the most famous in Oman and begins at the summit of Jebal Shams, a height of 3,005 metres. The barest of paths clings to the edges of the steep-sided canyon and past the abandoned village of As Sab, somehow perched on the edge of the cliff. One can only imagine what life must have been like for the inhabitants here going about their daily lives in such a dangerous location. As we made our way back along the route, watching every footstep, most of them perilously close to the cliff edge and a drop of hundreds of feet, we'd gathered some of the spectacular gnarled branches that littered our path. The Oman countryside was sprinkled with these parched tree branches and evidence of the struggle for water in this dry land. The boys, in their customary obliging fashion and familiar with my sometimes irregular requests, offered to burden themselves and negotiate the route back, loaded with these great if not unwieldy specimens.

It brought a smile to my face seeing the kind man, now carefully wrap the branches in packing paper and slot them into one or two of the rare gaps between the boxes. I'd felt a tug. In spite of all of the emotional derailment that coursed through the few years as aggressively as the Oman dried-up river beds, or Wadis, swathed their unrelenting way, carving paths through almost impenetrable rock, we'd had some genuine good times with the family. I also realised how much I loved the country, the Sultanate of Oman, and the great warmth of the people there as friendly as I've ever encountered. I wondered if we'd ever be back.

The predicted arrival date of our belongings, after months of promises and dates that failed to produce anything, unfortunately coincided with my arrival back to Gabon from a short UK school holiday trip. Bizarrely, I'd sat on the little connection flight taking us the final leg from Libreville to the Yenzi camp beside a Scottish girl. I'd noticed her in the tiny departure, arrival and baggage collection room whilst we were waiting to board our flight from Libreville. She was with a group of similarly clad outdoor khaki-types and closer inspection revealed that members of her team were straining to support heavy bags of cameras and filming equipment. Fore-warned that there was a BBC team arriving in the area to film a wildlife documentary, it didn't take many moments for me to piece things together. A couple of fellow travellers, whom I knew to be contractors making the regular monthly trips from Europe to Gabon, stood with me in line to have our baggage weighed ahead of it being wheeled out to our tiny `plane. As far as I could see, apart from the unusual gathering of so many British people in the BBC team, we were the only other Brits in the room and, more than likely, in French Gabon's diminutive departure hall, the only English speakers. We gestured greetings to the visitors, though unwilling to relinquish our position in the queue and somehow awkward at the unex-pected presence of so many of our fellow countrymen in this strange place.

Handing over my reusable and tatty, laminated boarding pass to the flight attendant at the foot of the few steps up to the `plane, I climbed the steps and set about trying to fit my bags into the limited space available in compact overhead lockers. I sighed deeply in relief to be on the final leg of my trip after an overnight stay in Paris and an overnight stay in Libreville. Minutes later I noticed the female member of the British film crew make her way down the aisle. "Do you mind if I sit here?" she politely asked in her steady, confident Scottish tones.

"No, not at all," I replied, simultaneously advising her of the best solu-tions for packing away oversized hand luggage in undersized compart-ments.

I listened fascinated during the flight to her detailed plans for the doc-umentary she was to be filming. She and her colleagues were to be living out in the open, in a tree house that had been specially built by a British survival expert. The plan was to live amidst the monkeys of Gabon and integrate as wholly as possible with nature. Something in her conversation began to sow a seed of discontent in my head. I sensed in myself almost a fear of opening our newly arrived container and facing up to 'normal life'. I even began to wonder if my resistance to this prospect had played some part in our container taking three times the usual transit time. Deep down I knew that the thing I was really searching for wasn't something that I could simply unwrap from its cardboard mummification. Material possessions would add to our home comfort but would do nothing to enrich the soul. The Scottish doctor and I parted company moments after I'd hauled my two bulging overtly western suitcases off the tiny roller belt at our little outdoors arrival area on the camp. "Good luck," I shouted, as she walked away. "I'll be thinking about you."

"Thanks very much, it's been nice to meet you," she offered back. I watched her stroll off as she swung her small canvas rucksack over her shoulder and she and her team packed themselves and the filming equipment into two 4 x 4 cars and headed off on their adventure.

I struggled my suitcases into the boot of our car and made my way back to the house. Feeling overwhelming guilt at the prospect of living in an air-conditioned house, I hadn't pointed out the rusting container parked outside our house as we'd flown over the camp on the final descent to the airstrip. I felt so pampered and appalled by the contrast between this lady from my homeland and I, that on sight of the container coming into view through the tiny window on the `plane, I'd made a fuss about the lagoon that is nestled in the centre of the camp and directed her eyes slightly north-east to that instead. I didn't need to add insult to the injury.

As our car turned the corner into Monkey Road there it was, as incongruous as any other metal monstrosity I'd seen in this quiet land. It was definitely rusty but fortunately not more rusty, I believed, than the last time we'd seen it. The closer I got, the more I began to wonder why on Earth we'd felt it necessary to fill such a massive vessel and, more worryingly, how we were going to fit it into the house when it appeared to dwarf the dimensions of the building.

The container seal was quickly inspected and the Customs official took her seat adjacent to watch for any items liable for duty. Firstly the gnarled sticks were extracted from the freight container's metallic jaws and then, one by one, the various boxes and swaddled furniture were carried out on the backs of exhausted men, until all that was left inside the container was silence. It was as though there had been a party in full swing with music and cheer, and then a festive balloon popped and in an instant it was all over, five hundred guests, tables and bands magicked away leaving pure, clear silence and calm. We hadn't even been asked to pay duty on our goods and the Customs lady promptly left, thanking us for the tea and biscuits supplied frequently to her little stool under the mango tree.

The riots and revelling had now begun inside 120 Monkey Road, hundreds of boxes and wrapped items seemed all to be screaming with the greatest urgency for attention and to be opened. The loudest and most desperate sound, though, was in my own head and as I plunged my little knife into the first carton, ripping its parcel tape seal, I thought of the doctor in her tree house, living her passion and carrying out her life's mission. It was almost as if I was turning the blade inwards on myself, frustrated at the sense of lack and aching at not following my own life's mission fully.

I channelled the angst rising in my every pore towards getting the task of unpacking done as swiftly as possible and ridding the house of the mountain of packing materials accumulating. I amazed myself at the energy I managed to summon and the strength to handle items that would normally have presented themselves too weighty for my slight frame to deal with. I clambered over boxes piled to the ceiling in search of the next logical box to open. I opened chests of drawers and wardrobes and somehow managed to waltz my way with them through fields of debris, room by room and into their approximate new positions. At times I felt the full futility of the task at hand and the more belongings I uncovered and the more the house filled up, the more the reality of so many possessions intensified my empty despair.

As seasoned travellers we know this unpacking normally symbolises a true arrival in a location. So many fantasies have passed furrowed and unsettled brows of how great life will be once reunited with one's personal effects. As I tried to make some sense of why I wasn't feeling the joy I'd felt on previous occasions with this great unpack it occurred to me that I'd had plenty of early indications rising of discontent to come. I remember the days and nights spent shopping and preparing for this minute and the feeling that something in me was out of alignment, even way back then. Many of our trips to stock up on the basic 'essentials' for our life in Gabon took us into the areas of Oman beyond the plushness of the capital Muscat, and into areas where it was easy to see people living way below our own affluent means. Indeed, we knew many of the sales people assisting us out to our car burdened by bathroom cabinets, wood, hoses and the like were separated from their families for years at a time, working overseas to make money to provide a better quality of life for their families back home. Our own fortune and emphasis on placing so much of self in these 'things' embarrassed and disgusted me. It seemed so at loggerheads with the inner peace and spirituality I sought and this notion that in ourselves we are complete.

It didn't take long for our African house to take on the flavour of our last abode. Sofas rested their heavy feet on familiar rugs and cushions reacquainted themselves with friendly chairs. The sparkly crystal candlesticks, high on my list of important boxes to open early and buried beneath boxes of mundane and heavy paper materials and cookery books, looked beautiful spreading their optimistic light into the room.

At times like this, with spirits flat, their shine and the way they brought the light of the outdoors into the middle of the room before projecting it so dazzlingly around the walls had the ability to grab my focus entirely. Several times I caught myself mesmerized by this ability of theirs to bring the light to the shadows as they did. I'd take myself completely away from my own torment and appreciated the momentary peace and the wonder of the perfect moment.

I began to make more sense of the discontent both my husband and I had found in our settling in Gabon. Back in Oman almost a year ago the preparations and lengthy visa wait before embarking on this move had allowed us to be completely swallowed up by being busy. If we weren't actually engaged in the physical preparation side of the move, our minds were certainly never still or quiet, nor at peace. On rising and on waking we were caught up in the 'to-dos' and the whens of visa arrival and hows of the life ahead and we completely forgot to centre ourselves. I can recall being too unsettled even to paint, the one thing I know, where I can be so present that life's urgencies aren't able to distract me. Dog walks were fitted in instead of enjoyed and generally we were never without our lists. Not for a moment.

So great had our list-making and ticking and adding-to become that, almost bizarrely, my husband now carried everywhere with him a clip-board, with sheets of paper subdivided into categories of tasks. As well as the practical lists - kitchen, stationery, hobbies, Travis and so on - this board listed the paperwork formalities and form-chasing which as ex-pats we are somewhat used to, but which is always stressful. We had the visits to the vets, local and airport vet and co-ordinated injection programme for Travis. We'd had all of the paperwork translated into French. Second-hand motor bikes, bought in Oman to provide a new hobby option for jungle living, needed even more documentation than Travis. We had to satisfy the Oman authorities that the export was in order and have the vehicles licensed for this purpose. We had to undergo the customary medicals for leaving one destination as well as having our arms pierced like pincushions to protect us from African diseases, bites and so forth. In addition we had the unfortunate visa delay for my husband's new work permit, keeping us under enormous strain and enough to impact on a serene moment, never mind the rest of our logistical nightmare.

✳

I now see that we arrived in Gabon at complete odds with ourselves. It's no wonder we found things to be so tough and the place to feel so unfriendly and un-accepting of us new arrivals. To exacerbate this we'd gone from chaos and not a moment of stillness engulfed by the pre-departure action list, to a bare house in a location where it was even impossible to take yourself out for a simple coffee. It was quite understandable that the unfriendly vibes we sensed were merely exacerbating our frail conditions and that we were functioning in a compromised state. It is impossible to find contentment in any area of your life from the base of rampaging unhappiness. The energy that you emit to the world is the one that is reflected back at you. Lack of appreciation of this concept is the reason may people feel under attack and misunderstood by the people surround-ing them. To an extent, I see the same phenomenon played out in many new arrivals and you know they have some reintroductions to make with themselves before any of the fitting in and socialising gets easier.

✻

One by one boxes were emptied and the flattened cardboard was given out to those who were queuing and appreciative. A container's arrival is always known to yield bonuses and this was particularly the case for our little sea-and-lagoon-locked camp where it was a challenge to find anything much at all. Inevitably there are packed items that don't fit into new surroundings. A cushion or chair that held its own splendour in a previous posting can suddenly be exposed for its weaknesses, for its lack of comfort or overly faded hues. In a place like Gabon, where there are so many people in need and the sense that small donations of this ilk can make big differences to people less fortunate, it is even more rewarding to give away your material excesses. After two weeks of solid, unabated unpacking and arranging, I left to join our youngest son for his final school half-term break and with a heaviness in my head and heart and uncertainty about what it was that I needed.

Chapter 14

Ageing Parents and Flights Home

The inevitability of ageing parents and ill-health was to be the next upheaval for us in Gabon. One Sunday morning, alarmingly early, the `phone rang. It was my father-in-law bearing the news that my husband's mother had passed away. She'd been very ill for some months now but nevertheless the notion that she hadn't won her battle for life had come as a complete shock. I think at these times, as I remember when looking into the dying face of my dad, although there is a degree of shock at the tragic outcome there is also a knowing that the end was inevitable. We knew as we looked into his eyes that there was no point of return from such illness for him. The heart knows but the mind refuses to acknowledge these long sad farewells.

That morning in Gabon, it was as though an electric blender had pulsated through our house and emotions, understandably, were running high. Barely able to process the shocking news, my husband immediately set about trying to get a flight out of our camp, a seemingly impossible task at such short notice. In his favour, he already had the required exit visa in his passport, without which no amount of vacant seats on an international flight would be of any use to him.

❋

Perhaps with some sense of what was to transpire, several days earlier my husband and I had gone to the village police station, which consisted of no more than a large, bare reception room with a mahogany desk and a scattering of miscellaneous wooden benches for attendees to wait whilst exit-visas were processed. The chief of police and his assistant, whose job it was to deal with the rudiments of finger printing and photo-taking, were concealed behind two closed doors and every eye in the room was trained on them for any signs of action. This necessity of visa formalities was always a tedious precursor to a trip out of the camp. On this particular occasion, as if to highlight the tensions in our household of a parent in such poor health and the rising, associated emotions, the African sky was black and the rain made the short drive over the pot-holes in road surfaces even more difficult than usual to negotiate. I'd not been able to find a ray of brightness internally or externally or a glint of finding any sort of peace and acceptance of the increasingly difficult situation.

We'd entered the police station passing a local girl, the acting reception-ist with her head in her folded arms, rested on the wooden desk and fast asleep. Our quiet shuffle past her wasn't enough to rouse her or stir any curiosity from her slumber. It was common to find the receptionists and authorities alike either asleep or deeply intent in a game of solitaire on aged computers, resenting the interruptions to their game that a customer such as us created. With our moods low however, on this occasion the scene seemed even more depressing and matched the bleakness of the weather outside. We waited in the cold room, with its clattering air conditioner, for the nod from the processing room and, in turn, my husband and I sat in silence for our photos to be taken and were unresponsive to the pulling and tugging and pressing of our fingers onto the tiny fingerprinting pad by the police officer.

We left the room and exited into the lightness of the air outside. Even the bleak weather was better than the stagnant energy of the police station and the interactions with local people who had failed even to raise a "Bonjour" to match the ones we offered. Indeed, the policeman had barely made eye contact with us, never mind offering a verbal greeting. We drove home, low and miserably deflated.

I'd always struggled with the melancholy vibe that emanated from Gabon. I could never quite put my finger on the source of it but it was constantly palpable and deeply unsettling to me. I felt it either had to be a result of a deep-seated resentment of us transiting foreigners to the country, which I could perhaps understand, or something to do with the dark energy associated with the Bwiti religious following that conjured up a pervading negativity. This animosity I always sensed from many of the local people I met would totally drain me. In previous locations the spirit of the place and the warmth of our welcome had always been pleasurable and it made me sad to see the missed opportunities of this insular little African location. I'd sensed the energy of the place was depressed from the minute my feet touched down from the `plane wheels and noted that if I didn't make sure I kept myself in my own world of creative bliss, where nothing else really mattered, I would slip into lows myself.

After several international and local calls over a period of two hours, my husband managed to get himself seats on both our tiny local `plane as well as the international carrier that was to take him back to Europe. Remarkably, barely five hours after the sad news broke, he was on his way back to his family to support each other, now bonded in grief. I found myself alone in the jungle and slipping into a spiralling desperation.

✳

As events had transpired, I'd sadly been out of contact with both of my husband's parents and his sister and her family for more than seven years. What with a parallel estrangement with my twin and her family since my dad's death, many times I'd had to fight hard to convince myself that the problem wasn't my undesirable company. Fully aware that communication is a two-way process, I could at any time in that period of estrangement with my in-laws have tried to initiate some reconnection from my side. Instead, I'd left the impasse as it was and tried to make the best of coping with the dysfunctional family dynamics and the ongoing sense of injustice. In the UK, my husband occasionally visited his family with our two boys and this awkward and awful scenario wounded me on every occasion. The general idea that this seemed to be an acceptable thing to do added small slices of pain to the deeper hurt I was already feeling about the whole sorry mess. I couldn't understand why I needed this relationship punishment.

My in-laws and I had not had any grand falling out. On the contrary, my last visit to the family years ago was to check on their well-being at a time when my husband was immersed in a mid-life low. I manage now to look on the cessation of his family's contact with me as a culmination of people being thrown into embarrassed chaos and just not knowing what to do or how to deal with the hurting people around. Unsure, his family had stood frozen in a silence that grew from weeks to years.

I've the utmost respect for people who extend caring hands to people; people who pick up `phones and write cards and letters to those, like me at the time, who are in need of a sign of someone on this Earth who cares. In many ways having a son in a vulnerable state allowed his parents to rise up certainly more than they had been able to do in previous years and to nurture their child once more as they tried to steer him back to himself. In the case of sons, perhaps society and the sons themselves feel the need to grow up strong and fast and the parental role quickly and abruptly becomes very much a passive thing, with neither party wanting to step over lines. The chaotic scenario presented them with a golden opportunity to demonstrate their love for their son which was a silver lining to such a dark storm. Nevertheless, I'd felt cast as the enemy and the suffering was unbearable at times. I'm able to recall and write about this now without the physical ache to the stomach and solar plexus that I became accustomed to living with for years. I always felt that the communication and behavioural errors were something my husband should have attempted to try to fix as fully as he'd allowed the situation to go awry. It was taking me all my energy just to survive and I'd no reserves left to act as peacemaker or even to know whether any of my intervention would have alienated me further.

After my husband left Gabon to be with his bereaved family, the only thing that persuaded me to make any trips out of the house on Monkey Road was the need to walk Travis. I knew everything about my person looked and felt broken and I really couldn't face the scrutiny of others that happens in these enclosed locations. Sure enough, people began to look at me bewildered and were particularly confused as to why I was still there in Africa when there had been a family death and impending funeral. Although they didn't say it, oblivious to any history, I sensed their harsh judgement and I knew it wasn't an appropriate time, if ever there was one, to enlighten them into my side of things. I could almost feel the buzz of excitement rising from the dullness of the camp and knew that we'd given them another topic to discuss other than the latest elephant tale.

It was a desperate period for me and easily the bottom of a hole I never wish to slip into again. Even the destruction to mind and body of the South American posting and the immediate fall-out from that paled in comparison to the low I now found myself in. It was as if all the lows ever encountered had culminated in this moment of hopelessness. I struggled on for three days, without hearing a word from home of how plans were going and how people were doing and, despite my estrangement from my husband's family, it would have taken a very closed down soul not to have cared how the family, especially my husband and sons, were coping. I angrily threw all of my many spiritual books into a cupboard. Banished. I felt I'd been doing everything I could to get back on track from the derailments in my life. In those bleak few days in Gabon I truly felt a nothingness beyond myself. My faith in guardian angels and inspirational, protective beings was all but lost. I needed a hug and to hear reassurance and support but the air felt black and empty around me.

Eventually I booked myself a flight out of Gabon. I knew this was going to be a serious trip and I had the feeling that I'd not be back in the jungle for a long time, if at all. I'd reached the end of my being able to cope with years of discontent and the end of being able to tolerate the dysfunction, as I saw it, of others. I didn't know what my plans were for the UK but I knew I needed to summon up the strength finally to take life on and find a way not only to get out of the hole I was in but to be able to stand on the mountain tops complete and whole. Life on Earth is brief and certainly too short to keep on making the same errors and sacrificing myself to fit in with the rules of the 'trailing spouse' that keep boats steady, but souls out of sync with themselves. I knew I needed more from life and conjuring up the best dinner parties and being an exemplary hostess were not the areas where I'd find my complete contentment.

I made plans to have Travis looked after. One of the fortunate things about Gabon was that idea that dog-owners helped each other by dog-sitting during absences from the camp. I was heart-broken leaving Travis, even though I knew he would be well taken care of and enjoy the company of his canine chum, a faithful little Lhasa Apso with a very loving heart. I thought back over how many years I'd contemplated an extended trip away like this but had never had the courage to separate from this wonderful little dog of ours. He'd always been able to sense our discontent and had soothed and transmuted a multitude of family pains. I will forever be indebted to him. As I packed to leave I decided to strip some of my canvases off their wooden stretchers and, as I'd done on many an occasion, rolled and slotted them into sections in my golf bag. Sadly, in Gabon this was the first time my golf bag was put to any use. Though drained, by now I'd found a bubble of increased energy and had managed somehow to tackle the practical side of looking through my belongings and selecting whatever I felt was important into my suitcase, taking breaks when the emotional enormity of my packing overwhelmed me.

I can't recall great details of flying out of the camp. I think I was so shut down, traumatised and exhausted by then that I had little capacity for reflection. I don't remember looking back at the camp as I normally did, when the tiny `plane lifted me off the ground and airborne. Mercifully, the long haul flight from Libreville to Paris passed without incident and as I stood in Paris, awaiting passport checks and chatting to one of the other passengers, I felt an inkling of some strength returning. At some level a part of me recognised the enormity of the decision I'd just made and importantly had acted on. It had taken every bit of my courage to listen to the little voice that had been urging me for so many years to do what would make me happy whatever the consequences. This wasn't just rocking boats, it felt like blasting holes that would have them struggling to remain afloat. I had no idea what the repercussions would be.

My arrival back at Edinburgh airport, laden with my heavy suitcase and golf bag containing my rolled up canvases, felt immediately strange. For all our years of overseas life, we'd been in the habit of coming home with virtually empty cases to ensure that there was plenty of capacity to pack all the UK items to take back that were unavailable in our foreign locations. Nigeria and Gabon were particularly challenging in this respect and most times we'd stock up on everything from frozen meat and new printer ink cartridges to potatoes, green beans and spare motorbike parts. We always had to prioritise our luggage on arrival at the small domestic airports that lifted us to our African camps. Often, either luggage capacity or fuel was limited, and as such it frequently took several days before belongings made it to the camp. It was always imperative to make the food case the top priority and always incredibly satisfying to have transported such basic treats to cheer up remote locations. I remember prior to one Scottish Burns Night in Nigeria, the suitcase containing the haggis had gone missing, suspected to be en-route for the Far East. We never did get to the bottom of the mysterious location of the Scottish delicacy, nor were we able to serve haggis that year.

✳

In Oman, during the days of old technology and bulky videos, it was mandatory that suitcases were x-rayed to check for evidence of videos prior to being allowed to leave the Arrivals Hall. In accordance with the country restrictions, videos had to be handed over to Customs officers and would be returned some weeks later after having any risqué scenes edited. Needless to say, people went to great lengths to try to circumnavigate this procedure and somehow to reach their foreign homes with fresh, unadulterated latest releases. I remember one friend in particular who had devised an elaborate strategy for the import of his videos into the country. He'd worked out that the ideal way to get his movies past the scrutiny of the x-ray machine and its able if not somewhat over-zealous analysers, was to make aluminium footprints of shoes and stick one to each side of a regular shoe box. After that, he removed the video tape from its housing and stored the reels of footage, from terrifying thrillers and BBC dramas to the most coveted children's cartoons, between the metallic footprints. He was confident that this would allow his videos to pass undetected through scanning.

I have memories of regular movie evenings hosted by this couple, which makes me think that there was indeed method in his apparent madness. In the later years video censorship became artful and sophisticated, and instead of a frozen scene marking where original footage had frustratingly been removed, elaborate car adverts and eagles flying round cliffs would be substituted for the removal of crucial sections of movies and plots. On our latest posting to Oman, technology had advanced even further with the rise in popularity of DVDs, making it impossible to apply the requisite censorship to inappropriate individual scenes and forcing the banning of specific DVDs instead. Magazines and newspapers also came in for censorship and in these cases inappropriate images were thickly obscured by permanent black marker pens. At times the pen marks would be hurriedly executed, obscuring the offending image and half of the accompanying text. Occasionally however, you'd come across a publication where the image masking had been done with painstaking care and attention and some evidence of artistic talent. Advertisements for sun tan lotions made more modest with the application of black marker strokes were sometimes shaded to resemble lace stoles and crocheted bikini-type tops and perhaps indicating a missed opportunity for a career in the fashion industry. Although this censorship concept may sound strange, it was never a huge issue for us and most of us were happy to oblige our gentle and polite Omani hosts. Maybe some of us understood what was deemed distasteful and admired the stance.

Exhausted from the days of wretched emotions and fear of what was to come, I arrived home in my taxi from Edinburgh airport to an empty house, my husband and our two boys having already left to attend the funeral. This period was immeasurably difficult and although my support for my bereaved husband came easily, we were miles apart in our distance. Whilst he and his family rallied and bolstered each other through their grief, I felt unwelcome and alone. I tried to keep myself out of sight as much as I could, taking myself off to quiet places like the old art galleries of Edinburgh and Glasgow, where one is left in peace to wander detached from life, without the raising of an eyebrow. Many times tears would roll down my face thankfully unnoticed, amidst the grandeur of the great and elaborate art surrounding me in these celebrated galleries. You always get the sense when viewing such imposing art that many emotions have already been involved and integrated with the paint from the thousands of viewers as well as the artist himself, who you felt had resolved and released many an internal sorrow in the creation of his canvas wonder. I know and understand from experience that this is exactly how art and the essence of creativity work.

Chapter 15

Introducing Fergus

The few days and weeks after the funeral were harrowing for us all in our different ways. Eventually, there came a point where my husband had been in the UK for the limited bereavement period his company permitted and there was nothing else for it but for him to return to Gabon. To my husband's great shock I conveyed to him my wish to stay longer in the UK. Indefinitely. He had assumed that despite our gripping tensions I would take my place in the drama and act out my spousely role as I'd been doing for so many years. As the words had left my mouth I felt a deep knowing that this decision was for the best and amidst my emotional fears I could sense my soul breathing a deep sigh of relief.

In the weeks that followed I spent a great deal of time on my own. I felt physically and emotionally at my lowest ebb and not inclined to see people socially or much at all. I began, however, to make regular trips to a dear lady, Shirley, a Reiki healer with the extraordinary ability to channel spiritual guidance. I'd occasionally sought her divine guidance over the years, but I sensed that this was a crossroads in my life and I needed support in finding the right path. I was facing the continuum of living at odds with myself or taking steps towards more completeness. I've always been fascinated with the concept of guardian angels and spiritual helpers and was absolutely open to anything that was going to set me back on my feet. Shirley remains one of the special people I've had the pleasure of meeting in my life who appear more as Earth angels than mere humans. A truly beautiful and caring soul.

Shirley's gift reached into dimensions beyond my own level of Reiki and she was regularly able to convey to me guidance and love from the wonderful world that is beyond sensing for most of us.

Angels and guides would regularly pop into these sessions and send messages to me via Shirley. Most often amidst a flurry of my tissues and tears I would be overcome with the love that was being directed towards me, particularly at a time when I couldn't make sense of many of my Earthly relationships. I could only describe the consulting room as full of pink love. Each time after these sessions I'd head home lifted and full of hope with the love and support I'd received in these divine messages and the way Shirley conveyed them so compassionately and with her amazing sense of humour. On occasions, as I made the thirty minute walk back to my house, it was all I could do not to punch the air in delight and out of pure happiness. Such a demonstration of joy would certainly not have gone unnoticed in Edinburgh's reserved but beautiful New Town and I normally fed this urge with a deep smile instead. With each session I had increasing feelings that there is more to life than simply the passage of years and events and meetings and partings that so many assume is the sum total. It became crystal clear to me that we have all agreed to missions whilst here on Earth and these times of struggle and devastation I was going through could be catalysts for making changes to unhealthy belief systems that were hindering the flow of my life and responsible for keeping me at the foot of the mountain, exhausted and bumping into the same sharp rocks, instead of being able to negotiate my way towards the summit.

Very often my dear dad would be present at these healing sessions, offering unwavering non-judgemental support for myself and also for the family he'd left behind. Shirley would pass on his comments to me along with his precise phrases and terminology as well as his sense of wisdom and tenderness that I missed so much in the physical since his passing at 59. Shirley was so incredibly intuitive that she was able to sense physical blocks of energy in my body and was able to help to move them from my stressed system, using the healing that was channelling through her from the angelic realms. At these moments I was often able to feel an intense heat or pressure as the healing worked its magic, and often sensed an array of wonderful colours.

It became evident during my sessions that my own mind was creating all that was happening in my life and that the most powerful way to begin to create more positive outcomes was to think more positively within myself. Our inner thoughts are what we live out and what manifest in our life. It's that simple. Changing and rewiring a lifetime of negative self-talk is achieved by painstaking and fastidious work. It was hard going, impossible at times and only this angelic guidance gave me the strength and faith to carry on with the task. Many of us live with the notion that life is something that happens to us and as such the highs and the lows are somehow sent to us without our control or permission. It's very easy in times of hardship to focus only on the sorrow, blame the universe for dealing cruel blows and to overlook the positive lessons that are always present no matter what the cloud. I began to see how wrong my previous attitude was and how much this hindered real forward momentum and positivity. I've learned also that our lows are our greatest gifts for teaching and for reflection. Something can only make us low if it somehow resonates at loggerheads with how we wish things and life to be. It's a bit like having already glimpsed your future as a trailer in the cinema and the distance the present feels from that is the measure of whether issues lift you to the sky or crush you to the floor.

This concept is something I have often had to apply to my art in a field that is notorious for its challenge and rejection. I used to get very low at the sense that I wasn't somehow breaking through into acceptance in the art world and being able to reach a larger world audience with my paintings. I've received immense help and encouragement from my heavenly helpers, working through this idea that my art hasn't yet been viewed in the capacity I really wish for. Ultimately, from the Heavens, I received guidance that "To paint because you love to paint and not for any viewing, sales or recognition agenda, will result in a special purity of work where at the deepest level creativity is Heaven-sent." It's as if art becomes part of creation itself. It doesn't get much more wonderful than that. I'd immediately understood the message and felt distinctly shame-faced at my human egotistical viewpoint and my impatience. Guidance is always delivered with compassion and often incredible humour and even powerful revelations like this can be completely and easily absorbed and understood in all their potency.

I've had technical, celestial discussions about the use of certain colours and instructions on the build-up of layers. At these sessions, I've even remarkably 'spoken' with one of the great painting masters, and one of my particular favourites, Matisse. Via Shirley my amazing Earth angel, who knew nothing of this great master, I listened speechless to Matisse talk about his love of the particular shade of blue he used and of the many years of his own frustration and years of rejection, trying to find exposure for his work. He explained that he was ahead of his time and understood my frustration and said it was a matter of one individual seeing something unique in the work, and from that a following begins. I was heartened to hear his verdict that the same thing would happen to me. Shirley correctly sensed him in a wheelchair in his latter years and relayed the message that he had watched me working and that he liked the decisive way my brushes moved and that felt every brushstroke was applied with love.

I do believe I spilled tears of joy that day with such proof of the marvel of our human lives and how we are all connected in this matrix of energy and able to access realms that are around us. I believe any one of us can tap into the energies of past geniuses of their time and elicit tips and clues, from Einstein to Picasso. I've always had a sense of continuum and that a soul passing on Earth wasn't in any way the end of the end, but merely part of the continuing growth of the individual soul and as such souls that leave the Earth aren't gone forever and their knowledge and guidance can be accessed in quiet moments and times of meditation.

I've been encouraged and supported through all the bleakest art moments, including many nights spent crying in bed, releasing the build up of sheer art frustration and the lows of a hundred requests sent to galleries seeking exhibitions space for my work that failed to materialise as even a single reply in my email inbox. Lately, I have a growing conviction that this pursuit, where I spend my days in solitude stroking brushes of technicolour across my canvases, is absolutely my life's mission and a means for me to share a vision and love with the world. I cannot convey enough my joy in this concept of the angelic realms working alongside us and how rich my life has become from living with this knowledge base and asking for their loving guidance. There is comfort in knowing that not one of us stands alone, even when we feel abandoned, unloved and desperate. At every moment, you can be assured and comforted. Despite not being able to see them, our guardian angels are whispering words of encouragement in our ears and bathing us in unconditional love. Our job and our challenge, and it's a big one, is to be still in our minds and to try and sense their wisdom as inspiration that drops into our hearts and heads.

A belief in my artistic ability grew to the extent that I scheduled an exhibition of my work in a local gallery. My exhibition was titled appropriately 'Angel Wings in Bloom', the title of a small painting I'd done in Africa of a simple white lily, that turned out to have two clearly defined angel wings forming the petals of one of the flowers I'd painted. Instead of continuing my focus on what was wrong and where my life was incomplete, my exhibition preparation absorbed my total attention for several months. I was at times almost overwhelmed by the images that I wanted to paint for the exhibition as well as the business side of publicity, catering and invitations. I was hugely supported with this exhibition, almost as if people were being dropped into my lap to aid me with what could have felt like an overwhelming task. There was my amazing framer, a young guy with a visionary head, gentle, hard-working and with the perfect eye for co-ordinating a frame to bring out the best in a piece of work. He hand-stained every one of my frames with coloured bases and waxed top coats to pull out specific colour accent from the canvases. I had the most incredible support from one of Scotland's top interior design companies, who agreed to furnish the gallery in their edgy and funky style creating the ideal backdrop for my bold paintings. We had luxurious sofas and chairs decked with jewel-like velvet cushions that tied in with particular paintings. Luxurious rugs stretched themselves out over the wooden floor and gave the gallery space a grounded feeling, balancing the floor with the strength of the colours on the wall. There was a carved stone fireplace set against one of the walls and, in every corner, statues and obelisks added more than a hint of drama. I'd been keen to create a comfortable viewing space for people, mindful of an awkwardness that can come with entering stark gallery spaces, unnaturally devoid of furnishings. I had a tall eucalyptus installation that reached from floor to ceiling, not only adding a fantastic natural element but spreading its heady and beautiful aroma into all corners of the gallery. Outside, and in keeping with the title of my exhibition and keen to include my love for all things spiritual, I'd drawn angel wings which had been processed by a lighting company into a template which shone large and beautiful wings of light onto the ground at the entrance of the gallery. The scene had added warmth with a welcoming fuchsia pink light focused on the old stone walls of the Edinburgh gallery.

The exhibition was a success and in particular an amazing release of pressure, after such long times of art-frustration, to have been able to display my work in a setting that created a 3-dimensional sensory experience for people; from the visual, to the aromatic to the Heavenly music. It was important to me that the combination would stir something in the people who came to view the show. During the period of exhibition, I had the opportunity to get direct feedback from my audience and I was intrigued to hear many people comment on a particular energy they felt in my work. Indeed, and I'm sure not by mere coincidence, there had been a lot of like-minded and open souls who had come to the exhibition. Evidently many angels had been at work whispering into appropriate, receptive ears.

There is a sense that when one is exhibiting work that has taken, in my case, almost three years to produce that somehow as an artist this is a way of recording a specific period of working and that subsequent work will have a new and evolving feeling to it. This notion came clear to me as I began to work on some of my post-exhibition commissions. Subtly, I knew a change had happened and I drew some excitement from seeing the emergence of lighter backgrounds and much less use of my beloved moody dark shadows. I knew that although I didn't feel like 'a new person' something positive had shifted that was making its way into my work.

I know that over tumultuous years I've done a great deal of healing during my many hours of painting. There were times I remember my frustration with life and, as I saw it, life's unfairness had me shedding so many tears, that I'd had to take moments away from the easel to allow my eyes to clear enough to regain focus to resume painting. There were times too, at particular low points, that I had enough despair rising within me to take my left hand containing my brush and plough it entirely through the canvas, splitting the fabric and my weeks of work, hacking, slicing and stabbing until I felt a release from pent-up angst that was torturing me. Instead, I would maintain composure and work the tiniest brushes on the largest canvases for hours and days, weeks and months until the same release was achieved.

I recall the production of one painting in particular, whilst I was in Gabon and trying to lift myself out of the low I was in, where my decision to paint more of a landscape scene for a change, with leaves and a striking and optimistic blue sky, resulted in an almost entirely black canvas. Though terrified by the jungle and its frightening noises and indications of the life it contained inside that could at any point grab or hurt me, I'd taken myself off to walk amongst the trees and gain inspiration for the blank canvas that was sitting on my easel waiting quietly for direction. For the first few minutes I allowed my fear to dissipate and tuned into the strength of the leaves and trees surrounding me. Nestled at the foot of these giant trees were the most unexpected, delicate lilac flowers. I remember sensing a particular relief from their presence and the notion that if they felt safe in such a setting, then so must I.

Bravery rising, I'd ventured a little further until I was literally stopped in my tracks. In front of me was a thin, grey snake, almost two metres long with the front section of its body lifted from the ground and swaying menacingly at me. I was frozen with fear. This was possibly one of my all-time biggest fears, an encounter with a snake where one footstep closer would almost certainly have had the snake strike out. Somehow, I managed to deposit my foot, still suspended in the air and the nearest point of contact with the disturbed reptile, to the ground and gingerly began to take steps backwards. So slow was my retreat that I almost felt my heels moving separately as though disconnected from the toes in a motion not unlike that of the snake itself. The snake, sensing the danger passing, relaxed from its attack mode and was slithering quickly away into the undergrowth.

Back in the safety of my home, still shaken by my encounter, this incident hadn't helped my general demeanour nor my feeling of being entirely at loggerheads with this little jungle enclave we lived in. I took it as a sign that I wasn't welcome and later in the day began to paint. Gone were my intentions for the depiction of a blue, hope-filled sky and instead I began to work vigorously in mud tones and black. Instead of my normal love of building up fine layers over weeks, I'd decided to paint this work by the wet on wet and more speedy painting method and as such my brushes were quickly documenting my mood and disconnection within myself. Although not intentional, the painting has a turquoise area in it that immediately draws you in and almost looks like the eye of a snake, and I wonder if this was my subconscious keen to represent my serpent sitter.

The finished painting, entitled Snake Encounter: Gabon, was singled out by a few at my exhibition as being somewhat different to the rest of my work. Whilst not going into the full drama of the period and the chaotic life situation, I was at least able to explain to people my snake tale. Although this piece stands out alarmingly for its horror-filled drama, I stand by every single and individual brush stroke documented, every black and blacker black and every brilliant hue that managed to work its way to shine in the foreground. When art comes from the deepest reaches of your heart, there is no randomness to the selection of colours or the balance of light and dark. The canvas is an honest reflection of the artist's state of self-perception. I am able to look back on that piece and that encounter these days with perhaps more of a spiritual head. It could very well have been the final facing myself in the mirror and seeing how unhappy I was and summoning up the courage to face my fears head-on. I don't for a second think that snake wasn't sent to teach me something, literally to stop me in my tracks and instead of continuing lonely repetitions of days one after the other, to stamp my foot with a new authority and make a better life happen.

❋

Back in Edinburgh I continued to see a lightness and optimism seeping into my work that fascinated me. On the face of it I knew that I still had much work to do in the pursuit of a contentment level I wanted, but I was encouraged looking at the work that I was producing that at least small steps had been taken.

An artist's life, however, can at times be immersed overly in solitude and with the family all living apart I began to crave canine company. I missed our Jack Russell to the extent that the mere mention of his name was enough to bring me to tears. His absence created the largest of holes and I found myself entertaining thoughts of acquiring an Edinburgh dog, a studio dog. The final trigger was stumbling across a photo of Travis on a social networking site in the album of someone I didn't even know. It was as if I'd lost everything. Even Travis had become socially integrated into the Yenzi camp and the pictorial evidence, shining out of my laptop, showed him perched on the side of a canoe bracing his body for any imbalance to the boat. There were other photographs of him investigating the aromas of meat cooking on a beach barbeque and tentatively dipping his paws into the still sea that lapped the sand.

It felt in my heart that I saw the acquisition of a dog for myself in Edinburgh as the beginnings of me creating a life more permanently alone. This idea refused to budge from my head and no matter how much I tried to point out to myself the challenge of dog walking in a damp climate like Scotland the idea quickly gathered steam. It wasn't long before I was in talks with a dear lady over the `phone describing the scene around her living room as two mischievous pups ripped up an entire box of man-size tissues. It was no good trying to talk myself out of the idea. I was already committed to the good and the bad, the frustration and the fun, of a new four-legged friend coming to join me.

I set about acquiring the necessities I'd need for the arrival of a dog and some days later found myself rushing up the stairs of our Edinburgh basement, on one of our all too common wet mornings, to introduce myself to the smallest dog I'd ever seen. I'd named him Fergus, a little Maltese Terrier, and I hoped that somehow, despite the geographical challenge, he and Travis would become friends. I've a feeling dogs choose us every bit or even more than we choose them and all sorts of doors threw themselves open facilitating this union of Fergus and myself. He arrived from Manchester, kindly driven by the breeder's husband right to my doorstep in Edinburgh. I had been trying to find a way around the logistical side of me being such a distance from the breeder, but the universe had already found a solution.

Almost immediately, my solitude was the furthest thing from my mind and my time was now spent tending to the needs of my new little companion. Slowly he began to settle in and it wasn't long before his tiny 1.2 kilo frame would come trotting behind me every time I left the room. I marvelled at his diminutive stature and had long since put his new tartan dog bowls to the back of the cupboard in preference for two old china tea cups more befitting his petite frame. In size, he reminded me of one of the toy highland cows, bonnets on and tartan scarves at the neck, piled up in the baskets that adorn the outside of our tacky Scottish tourist shops with some luminous, hand-cut, starry cards displayed alongside pledging similar delights in the store.

There were certainly moments of supreme challenge with puppy-dom and I remember on more than one occasion telling myself that this would be the last time I put myself through the process of being the mother to a baby dog. I reflected on Travis's first few weeks and the total exhaustion I'd felt at the time. Unlike preparation for motherhood where your body is flooded with anticipatory hormones before arrival and calming ones after the arrival, there is no such maternal assistance for new puppy owners. I recognised the overwhelmed feeling from before and knew that it would pass and that Fergus's undoubted character would soon negate the downsides of again having a junior dog responsibility.

I had set up a corner in my studio with a bean bag and Fergus seemed to understand and accept that he would spend quiet time in this room as I passed the hours doing whatever it was that occupied me to such a depth. I tried to find a work-dog balance so that my needs in the creative department were fulfilled as well as the needs of a small dog and most of the time things worked out, but not always. My artistic pursuits are such that I can become almost panicky if life eats too greedily into my painting hours. Over the years I've made countless weak excuses to well-meaning friends asking me out for a coffee, lunch or whatever. At all times, the first consideration is how I'm going to get my painting time and I've frequently carved myself an isolated life to facilitate this great need of mine to be in peace and creatively occupied.

My husband continued to make trips to our house in Edinburgh according to his leave entitlement and although things were strained, we somehow managed to find enough respect for each other and allowed ourselves to be a bit vulnerable and drop our guards with one another. I was mindful of his bereaved status and how much pain is associated with that as well as his need to spend time with his widowed father. I tried to utilise the spiritual vision of life that I was slowly piecing together and most of all tried to find the essential unconditional qualities of love. It's very easy for us to criticise one another for what we perceive as failings and yet we are all doing the best we can with the resources we have at that moment. I believe most of us want harmony in life and it is our relationships with others, in particular with our family, which show us areas where we ourselves are lacking. From a peaceful and contented person, the outward flow is one of loving compassion and less confrontation.

Some months after Fergus's arrival it came to me like a feather floating down from the sky with a message, a deep knowing that it was time to move house. The feeling was strong, but more in the sense that I didn't want to move but knew it was a necessary step. The house took several months to sell and at the time completely consumed my thoughts. I tried to surrender into the best outcome for both my husband and me individually and had really no idea whether we would remain under the same roof following a sale. I recall the feeling of huge uncertainty for the future and in particular of finding a home with a room I could convert to a studio to work in. It seemed as if I was asking for a lot. At some level I believe there was still an issue with letting go of the past difficulties that the family had gone through that I still had to work on. I believe this was keeping me attached to the fabric of the house and delaying any sale. Eventually a sale transpired and very swiftly a move to a new house a mere five minutes walk away followed. Much like the transporting of belongings to third world countries, this exercise taught me how tricky it can be to fit human life into a spiritual ethos. We put so much store on accommodation of our Earthly requirements, that it's easy to lose sight of the truth of what a home is. Home is the moment when all stands still, the peaceful space that enfolds when I'm busy at my easel or watching the sunset play out its amber glow in the sky. Home is the intangible sense of living in the flow of one's life and without attachment and yet marrying this with the general rudiments of life is something that challenges many of us. Perhaps this perspective was somewhat out of focus for me during what seemed a long drawn-out sale period and the dreaded energy-zapping fear of the future element took up too much of my space.

Our new home immediately felt right and I thanked everyone I could both on this side of life and in the Heavens for bestowing on me such great fortune and such a fine residence with a perfect studio, located first door on the right on entering the house. The property is Georgian and steeped in the historical feel of the New Town in Edinburgh. I've always loved these streets and feel very much at one with the days-gone-by vibe of the place. Our house is a basement and lower basement and is entered by descending a flight of curved steps that take you increasingly further from street level and below the pavement with every step. The bedrooms and my studio are located on the first floor and a further flight of steps takes you deeper into the belly of the ground and to the living and kitchen areas. Many of Edinburgh's streets are on such an incline that properties such as ours have an element of surprise about them. Rather than the dark interior you might expect having taken oneself to such a depth from pavement level, our house to the rear is ground level and first floor. Regardless of the northerly aspect at the rear of the house, light flows easily in through the astragal windows. The rear of the house also has something of a secret garden with a countryside feel and a peace that comes as a pleasant surprise given our city centre location. The house and garden feel like a calm space and very near to 'home'.

My husband and I set about opening boxes, building beds and adding our personality to the renovated space, a job we both relish, and it wasn't long before I found myself standing in awe of how visually perfect the space was becoming. We'd chosen to de-clutter from the previous house retaining only enough to make things personal enough, but had shed a lot of our older furnishings. We'd opted to retain items that didn't encourage the mind to track back to years gone by and their ups and downs, but which were more of the moment and matched exactly how I wanted to live. It can be hard to break the habit of casting one's mind back to painful events and reliving and re-energising them and as a result keeping yourself stuck and melancholy. I knew from my own experience that I'd spent some years taking up the victim's mantle and shuddered at the waste of energy this had been and how much this had prevented me from making any emotional progress whatsoever. Sometimes there is an unexplained fear of living happily that sends us opening our wounds the very minute we feel lightness is beginning to emerge, instead of welcoming that lightness in like the sunshine and the chirping birds through an open window.

Unfortunately, within a few weeks of our move and three days before Christmas my husband's ailing dad passed away. Although there was certain relief that he was now at peace as he wanted and no longer suffering from the effects of ill-health, the sadness was immense. After years of estrangement, I had expressed my hope that he would be strong enough to cope with the numerous steps down into our house and that after some years of silence between us there could be a reconciliation. Maybe this knowledge was enough release for him and knowing that his son and grandchildren were unusually all together under one roof for the Christmas period instead of in different cities and continents, he surrendered his grip on life. This time, although I elected not to attend the funeral, keeping things the same as they had been at the time of his mum's funeral, my husband and I were strongly united. He is a stoic man, my husband, strong and reliable and he handled his overriding grief with great dignity and not a shred of pity for himself. The sadness was in sharp contrast to the seasonal cheer of shops and malls that had been emitting Christmas songs since October. To make things more harrowing, my husband had been the one who'd found his dad on the floor of his bedroom, a physical body that would take no more breaths or ever be able to smile the proud and loving smile of a father to his son. It was a hard time and I felt privileged to be on hand to support him in any way I could. There couldn't have been a greater contrast to the passing of his mum only eighteen months earlier when we were both somehow in prison cells of ourselves, locked up and shut down to each other.

We spent a quiet Christmas Day, the four of us - myself, my husband and two sons - and the simplest of days. I thought a lot about the commercial madness that had been escalating ahead of Christmas and how repelled and appalled I'd been to see the customary craziness of people running like worker ants to be stripped of as much money as the stores could extract from them. It struck me too how the season of goodwill had turned into such a commercial affair that people, like my husband, who were in the midst of a crisis, somehow didn't fit in to the merriment of the time of year. That particular Christmas was a poignant time and regardless of all the ups and downs and marital disconnection, the four of us shared what I will always look back on as a special day where each of us was able to demonstrate strength and love for one another as well as respect for all of the loved ones we'd lost. I can't help feeling that somewhere many of us have strayed way off the track with this celebration period. It doesn't seem right that we've become so focused on our own satisfaction that we fail to consider those for whom a simple gift of emotional support and kindness surpasses anything that could be contained in shiny wrapping paper and a red bow.

As soon as I began to settle into the new house, I was curious to see what effect the move would have on me as a person and what if anything would be translated to my paintings. As if to make the transition smoother, I was working on a painting mid-move and so some of the energy it radiated would be from the old house and some would be tapping into the new. It seemed as if already things had recalibrated and there was no mistaking increasing lightness and happiness amidst the brushstrokes. The first painting begun in the new studio was of a succulent plant, a Sempervivum, and I experienced a particularly magical moment that I will never forget whilst working on it. The painting has strong burgundy leaves, flecked with bright reds and pinks and violet and turquoise highlights. As I was working one day, rapidly and what felt at the time decisively, bringing white paint from the background to lick the edges of the leaves, I had an overriding feeling of a Heavenly presence as though I was no longer even holding the paintbrush in my own hands. It seemed as if I'd managed to get myself so involved in the piece and bringing in this light to the painting that I'd awoken the very essence of myself and for the briefest moments there was no separation from myself and the Heavens. The painting is titled A Godly Moment. Almost all of my work contains this white area nowadays and a merging of two worlds as I see it and as I feel it.

I continued to immerse myself in my art and tried not to get too caught up with extended family dramas. Just as I'd begun to meet my twin sister, from whom I'd been estranged since our dad's death some fifteen years previously, my relationship with my mum and younger sister all but imploded. At times it is hard to fathom that these close relationships are often the springboard for change, no matter what the cost. It became so important to me to live truthfully and stop the repetition of unhealthy family dynamics that the price of voicing my opinions and hurt was a separation. I wish them well on their paths, however, and have come to accept that there are times when the only way forward is to let go and follow our own direction, and who knows what the future may hold as far as reconciliations go.

Chapter 16

Looking Back and Looking Forwards

My journey brings me up to the present day and my new understanding on the significance of much of the troubled times and struggles I've experienced along the way. My tale is remarkable in the unusual and exotic experiences foreign living has provided, but at the root is a simple story of a lost, unhappy soul desperate to be at peace and make some sense of the chaos encountered along the way. My spiritual beliefs, including angelic messages and Heavenly encouragement, have played a significant part in lifting me from the depths of the valley to the top of the mountains. I'm aware that I'm still 'a work in progress' as we all are in our human reality and whilst we are in this life we will continue to be presented with opportunities that will challenge us and promote our growth. I understand this now with hindsight and how wrong my previous views and resentment and anger directed at an unco-operative universe were.

My art gathers pace and continues to thrill me with its evolution. I'm currently preparing for an exhibition that documents the two and a half years that have elapsed since my last show. The change in my paintings is dramatic for the lighter energy radiating from the canvases and an array of colours that have an other-worldly feel to them, chronicling what I see as a positive internal transformation in myself. Amazing synchronicities occur these days, with magazines giving me free art editorial coverage and the right people coming into my field of vision at timely moments. It truly feels as if I'm in some sort of flow these days with life. My husband, now based in Kuwait, comes home as often as his work permits and I've been able to take a few days off my painting to go out to support him there. He works hard and moans little about living in so much solitude out there. I have the greatest respect for the way he supports and has always supported my painting and for tolerating the compromise of us living in separate continents. Gone are the days when he'd come home from work to a sad and depressed wife, preoccupied by there having been no apples, oranges, cucumber, lettuce, chicken and potatoes for nearly a month in the Yenzi shop and how much the company was failing to support us.

Travis made his way to Edinburgh, after a quarantine period in France as house-guest of an English lady and with five other transiting dogs, in particular his friend Hamish also destined for Edinburgh from his former residency in Syria. Travis and Fergus seem to have a deepening bond and are happy to share me and the visiting family. Travis's little grey water dish, converted back to its original use, had been once more attached to his travel crate and filled with water for his flight from Libreville to Paris and eventually to the UK, but has been stored away for the time being. There was a temptation to sit it on a desk and re-awaken its other purpose, but these days are gone and there is no need for such a physical reminder of a troubled time.

I have a much to thank Gabon for. Maybe without the enormity of the task living there presented, I'd never have had the strength to stop the conveyor belt I was on or experience the happiness I do nowadays. The tree that had lost all its branches feels healthy and light, unburdened by the shedding of wood that had grown overly heavy. It's not been an overnight transformation and at times it has been almost an unbearable journey, but when one ray of sunshine begins to break through the clouds and then another and another the pace of recovery or rebirth quickens. I am grateful for all of the relationships that have tested and exposed me and grateful for being able to view each of them for the good that they have brought me. I see that our relationships with others are our best ways of showing us the relationship we have with ourselves, the good within and the element in us that could be better or closer to our truth.

The greatest thank you of all goes to my husband and sons for their patience and hanging in there until I found myself. I have an extraordinary family and learn from them every day. In the end, one of my core lessons has been about understanding the unconditional element to love and human relationships and the other has been about learning to live in alignment with myself and with what brings me fulfilment and peace. It may be surprising to find my story wasn't about a 'simple' marriage break-up, but of painfully stripping back beliefs to reveal a deeper understanding of the nature of relationships and, importantly, people giving each other a second chance. My husband and I have tested one another and been beyond the brink no doubt, but as I finished writing this concluding chapter it becomes clear to me that ours is also a love story. I have an entirely new vision of life and our missions in it and of a spiritual and greater picture that provides us challenges and opportunities for incredible personal growth. Through sharing my story I hope to encourage others to view their struggles and their relationships in a completely new and empowering light.

My husband and I have recently had a conversation about the possibility that maybe, after his posting in Kuwait, we will try to find a company location that fits all of our family's needs, as well as an open and safe area for Travis and Fergus and, importantly, somewhere to accommodate my studio. It could just be that the crates and water dishes are once more in service. There is no rush, but we will know what feels right and trust that the loving guidance of our guardian angels steers us home.

Lightning Source UK Ltd.
Milton Keynes UK
UKOW03f2329091213

222686UK00019B/1020/P